Office Administration

THE M & E HANDBOOK SERIES

Office Administration

J C Denyer
ACIS, AHA, MInst.AM, AMBIM

Revised by

A L Mugridge
BComm(Lond.), ACIS

*Formerly Principal Lecturer,
Business Studies Department,
Bristol Polytechnic*

FOURTH EDITION

Pitman Publishing
128 Long Acre, London WC2E 9AN

A Longman Group Company

First published 1965
Reprinted (with amendments) 1966
Reprinted 1967, 1968, 1969, 1970, 1971, 1972
Second edition 1973
Reprinted 1974, 1975, 1976, 1977
Third edition 1978
Reprinted 1980, 1981
Fourth edition 1982
Reprinted (with amendments) 1983
Reprinted by Pitman Publishing Ltd 1986, 1988

© Macdonald & Evans Ltd 1965, 1973, 1978, 1982

A CIP catalogue record for this book is available from
the British Library.

ISBN 0 7121 1540 4

Founding Editor: P. W. D. Redmond

Printed and bound in Great Britain by
Richard Clay Ltd, Bungay, Suffolk

Preface to the First Edition

This book is intended to be a concise guide to assist students sitting examinations in which Office Management or Secretarial Practice appears.

It is not intended to be a complete exposition of the subject, but only to give the salient features, in writing of organisation, personnel, office systems, office machines, etc.

Test questions have been included in the book, the answers to which are indicated by the relevant paragraph numbers inserted. While it is not possible to give sufficient text to answer every conceivable kind of question, the information in the book provides the student with basic knowledge which will enable him to deal with most examination questions, however phrased.

The questions at the end of each chapter are based on the syllabus requirements of the examinations of The Institute of Chartered Secretaries and Administrators; The Institute of Health Service Administrators; Institute of Administrative Management, and Chartered Institute of Management Accountants.

January 1965   JCD

Preface to the Fourth Edition

Much of the material in the third edition of this HANDBOOK in 1978 has required fundamental revision.

Acts of Parliament continue to introduce increasing complexities in Industrial Relations: PAYE procedure was changed on 6th April 1981; word-processing and microtechnology have led to a fundamental reappraisal of many long-established office systems. Many of the office machines and devices described in this HANDBOOK have already been displaced in large offices, although their use will continue in small offices and examination questions about them may still be set.

The need for the student to keep up-to-date was never greater. Textbooks are rapidly out of date—constant reference to professional journals, visits to exhibitions of office equipment, comparisons of the student's own daily experience with what he learns are all essential aspects of the study of Office Administration.

January 1982   ALM

Contents

PART ONE: ORGANISATION AND PERSONNEL

PART TWO: OFFICE EQUIPMENT

List of Illustrations

List of Tables

ORGANISATION AND PERSONNEL

CHAPTER I

Nature of Office Administration

1. Introduction. Office administration involves the combination of labour, in the form of clerical staff, with capital, in the form of environment and equipment, in the proportions which, properly directed and controlled, will achieve the purpose of the office in the most efficient way.

2. Function of the office. This is basically to provide a service of communication and record, and in detail:

(*a*) to receive information (e.g. quotations, time-sheets, orders, etc.);

(*b*) to record information (e.g. inventory, prices, personnel data, etc.);

(*c*) to arrange information (e.g. costing, accounting, statistics, etc.);

(*d*) to give information (e.g. sales invoices, estimates, etc.);

(*e*) to safeguard assets (e.g. care of cash, stocks, important documents, etc.). In this context adequate insurance is of great importance.

3. Function of the office in business.

(*a*) It is normally secondary in importance to the main purpose (substratum) of the business (e.g. factory production ranks before office administration).

(*b*) It is complementary to the substratum. Thus, it is impossible to continue working the factory for longer than a few days without the office to assess and pay the wages, or to obtain and pay for raw materials etc.

(*c*) It controls the factors of production, notably by managerial, personnel and budgetary controls.

4. Definition of an "office". Section 1 (2) of the Offices, Shops and Railway Premises Act 1963 provides:

(*a*) "office premises" means a building or part of a building, the sole or principal use of which is as an office or for office purposes;

(*b*) "office purposes" includes the purposes of administration, clerical work, handling money, and telephone and telegraph operating;

(*c*) "clerical work" includes writing, book-keeping, sorting papers, filing, typing, duplicating, machine calculating, drawing and the editorial preparation of matter for publication.

5. Aspects of office administration in the pursuit of efficiency.

(*a*) *Purpose*. It is of fundamental importance to define the purpose of an office or of each of its constituent parts.

(*b*) *Organisation*. This is the arrangement of staffing and the allocation of duties to the staff.

(*c*) *Method* (systems). This is the sequence of operations and how and where they are performed and within what time-scale.

(*d*) *Personnel*. This is concerned with the recruitment, placing, training, motivation, promotion and dismissal of staff.

(*e*) *Environment*. This includes the office building, the layout of the departments and the physical conditions.

(*f*) *Equipment*. This includes machines and devices to assist the performance of clerical work.

6. Duties of an office administrator.
His primary duty is that of directing and controlling an office in order that its purposes be achieved with maximum efficiency. The word "efficiency" connotes the required volume and quality of work and service within the required time, consistent with economical use of resources and with good human relations with the staff. The words "office administrator" are sometimes used instead of "office manager", although there is a real distinction between the two. To avoid confusion, the second term will not be used in this book.

An office administrator is also an office supervisor, although a supervisor is not necessarily an administrator.

7. Office supervisor.
An office supervisor is one who controls the clerical work of all, or part of, an office. He is normally subordinate to the office administrator.

(*a*) *Main duties*.
  (*i*) Giving instructions.
  (*ii*) Motivating, training and controlling the staff.
  (*iii*) Maintaining good human relations with the staff.
(*b*) *His duties with relation to the work*.
  (*i*) Planning the work of the section (especially difficult where

there is much absence because of illness or holidays).

(*ii*) Ensuring punctual performance of work.

(*iii*) Securing the accuracy and quality of work.

(*iv*) Co-ordinating work with other sections and departments.

(*v*) Distributing work fairly.

(*vi*) Developing and introducing new methods of doing work to improve efficiency.

(*c*) *His duties to his subordinates.*

(*i*) To train them.

(*ii*) To develop understudies (for holiday reliefs, during sickness, etc.).

(*iii*) To delegate responsibilities (not to be confused with delegation of authority).

(*iv*) To settle personal friction and compose quarrels among the staff.

(*v*) To be as generous with praise for good work as unsparing of criticism for shoddy work.

(*vi*) To maintain discipline, reprimanding where necessary.

(*vii*) To control the working of "flexible working hours".

(*d*) *His duties to his superiors and associates.*

(*i*) To accept full responsibility for the work of his own department.

(*ii*) To co-operate with other supervisors.

(*iii*) To permit, and to encourage, interchange of staff.

(*iv*) To explain, and to enforce, the company's policies.

8. Office administration as a specialist subject.

(*a*) In practice, each departmental head may administer his own office, although his own speciality may be accountancy, law, engineering, etc. In these cases, office administration is not a specialist skill in the company.

(*b*) There is a growing tendency, however, for appointments as office administrators to be offered to administrators, trained as such, with professional qualifications such as from the Institute of Chartered Secretaries and Administrators.

PROGRESS TEST 1

1. What are the basic functions of an office? (**2**)

2. How does the office control the factors of production? (**3**)

3. How does the Offices, Shops and Railway Premises Act 1963 define "clerical work"? (**4**)

4. What are the broad aspects of office administration which contribute to efficiency? **(5)**

5. By what criteria would you assess the efficiency of an office? **(6)**

6. "All administrators are supervisors, although not all supervisors are administrators." Explain. **(6, 7)**

7. What are the duties of a supervisor to his subordinates? **(7)**

8. Is office administration necessarily a specialised function? **(8)**

CHAPTER II

Office Organisation

1. Organisation.

(*a*) Organisation is the structure by means of which the activities of the enterprise are distributed among the personnel employed in its service.

(*b*) It also comprises formal interrelationships established among the personnel by virtue of those responsibilities.

It is the framework within which people act. To organise an office is to arrange the parts so that the whole works efficiently as one integrated body.

2. Organisation chart.
A typical organisation chart is as indicated in Fig. 1.

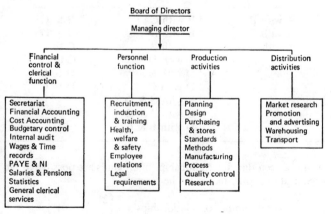

FIG. 1 *An organisation chart.*

The above chart is an example only. Every office administrator will draft the chart most appropriate to his own organisation. A correctly drafted chart is essential to a clear understanding of the scope of control exercised by the directors and their subordinates.

3. Principles of good organisation.

(*a*) There should be clear lines of authority running down from the top, with equally clear lines of responsibility running up from the bottom.

(*b*) The span of control (or span of responsibility) must be appropriate. That is, the span of supervising of an administrator over subordinate supervisors should not exceed his personal competence in controlling and co-ordinating their activities.

EXAMPLE: A is an office administrator with subordinates B, C and D directly responsible to him. Table 1 shows the relationships that are tenable.

TABLE I: Relationships between a superior and subordinates.

Direct single relationships	Direct group relationships. Consultation with one other, with others in attendance	Cross relationships
A with B	B with C	B to C
A with C	B with D	B to D
A with D	C with B	C to B
	C with D	C to D
A	D with B	D to B
	D with C	D to C
	B with C & D	
	C with B & D	
	D with B & C	

It can be seen that 18 relationships of all kinds are possible in the organisation, consistent with the formula:

$$\text{Total number of relationships} = n\left\{\frac{2^n}{2} + (n-1)\right\}$$

where n = number of subordinates: in the present example, n = 3.

Not all 18 of the theoretical relationships will necessarily be relevant in practice, but a sufficiently large number of them will apply, thereby complicating the responsibilities of the office administrator.

4. Delegation. This is the transfer of personal performance of duties to another, i.e. transferring power to make decisions or to take action. Although, in theory, only authority can be delegated, increasing activity in an organisation, which overloads administrators and supervisors, may, in practice, necessitate the delegation of some responsibility to lower levels in the direct line, or, preferably to specialists. Delegation, a difficult skill of administration, is a necessary function of centralisation.

5. Centralisation. This means that control is exercised from the centre, e.g. a head office issues instructions to branch offices and requires frequent, regular reports from them. In some cases, the accounting of the branch is done entirely at the head office: in others the branch carries out the accounting function for itself, the head office appearing as a major creditor in the branch books. The use of terminals within an electronic data processing system (EDP) greatly strengthens control at the centre, e.g. the payroll of a large factory in Scotland is prepared at the head office in London.

(*a*) *Advantages of centralisation.*

(*i*) More effective administrative control.

(*ii*) Easier handling of peak loads.

(*iii*) Supervision may conform to a standard.

(*iv*) More efficient use of equipment.

(*v*) Efficient deployment of specialist services, e.g. technical libraries.

(*vi*) Greater flexibility in the use of staff.

(*vii*) Economies in staff and equipment, e.g. centralised filing means fewer, but more expert, clerks, and less equipment than de-centralised filing.

(*viii*) Centralised holding of e.g. stocks of emergency stationery results in economy of total holding of these stocks—a familiar parallel with central holding of insurance funds.

(*b*) *Disadvantages.*

(*i*) Rigid control often resented by staff—suspicion of head office.

(*ii*) Tendency towards unnecessary bureaucracy, although this is not inevitable.

(*iii*) Dull uniformity in methods and repression of initiative.

(*iv*) Delays in flow of information and documents—"failure to communicate".

(*v*) Administrators tend to become remote and out of touch with working levels.

(*vi*) Work may be done in the order of receipt rather than in the order of importance.

6. Office services that can be centralised. While centralisation emphasises control from the centre, with office services it may mean, in addition, placing personnel in a central office, e.g. with a typing pool. The major services which lend themselves to this kind of centralisation are:

(*a*) dealing with incoming and outgoing mail;

(*b*) telephone, telegraph and communications generally, where central switchboards are a technical necessity;

(*c*) reception of callers, e.g. for payment of accounts;

(*d*) duplicating services;

(*e*) typing (typing pool or central typing department);

(*f*) filing and records;

(*g*) calculating;

(*h*) stationery and office supplies;

(*i*) forms control;

(*j*) office cleaning;

(*k*) canteen and refectory;

(*l*) employment and training;

(*m*) first aid.

7. The line type of organisation. This is where authority and responsibility flow in a direct line from top to bottom: where they are greatest at the top and taper at each successive lower level. Each individual is responsible to one senior person only.

(*a*) *Advantages.*

(*i*) Simple to understand and operate.

(*ii*) Clear-cut division of authority and responsibility.

(*iii*) Conducive to stability.

(*iv*) Discipline is easier to maintain.

(*v*) Executives have power and duty to act.

(*b*) *Disadvantages.*

(*i*) Tends to be rigid and inflexible.

(*ii*) Autocratic and potentially dictatorial.

(*iii*) May overload executives.

(*iv*) Departmental aims may displace company aims.

(*v*) Loss of an executive, i.e. a link in the chain, may be disastrous.

8. Functional (or lateral) organisation. Specialists are appointed to advise (or administer) a certain kind of work throughout the entire organisation. Emphasis is placed on their advisory function, authority being retained by the line officers.

(*a*) *Advantages.*

(*i*) Best use is made of commercial and technical expertise.

(*ii*) Better co-ordination.

(*iii*) Strengthens central control.

(*b*) *Disadvantages.*

(*i*) Conducive to overlapping authority, with consequent friction.

(*ii*) Employees may find there are "too many bosses".

(*iii*) Weakening of authority and initiative of supervisors.

(*iv*) May add to overheads with no corresponding contribution to efficiency.

9. Line and staff organisation. A combination of line and functional (lateral) types. While, in theory, it should combine the advantages of each, in practice it frequently inherits the disadvantages also. Its most serious fault is that of causing confusion for want of precise definition of duties.

10. Committee-type organisation. A management committee is assisted by a number of standing advisory committees (as in local authorities and hospital committees). Some form of line organisation is necessary in addition.

(*a*) *Advantages.*

(*i*) Many points of view can be marshalled—"so many men, so many minds".

(*ii*) Conducive to co-ordination.

(*iii*) A good medium for education and training.

(*iv*) Disseminates information.

(*v*) Makes use of specialists (especially by co-opting).

(*b*) *Disadvantages.*

(*i*) Expensive of the time of members—"a committee is a body that keeps minutes and wastes hours".

(*ii*) Some members may be unfamiliar with, or not directly concerned with, the agenda—"the things to be done". Not all chairmen are properly trained in committee procedure.

(*iii*) Action tends to be slow, and the outcome of compromise.

(*iv*) The authority of line officers is weakened.

(*v*) A weak chairman plays into the hand of aggressive committee members.

PROGRESS TEST 2

1. What do you understand by organisation? **(1)**
2. State two principles of good organisation. **(3)**
3. Delegation is a notoriously difficult action. Why? **(4)**
4. Discuss centralisation *v.* departmentalisation. **(5)**
5. What office services can be centralised? Which of these must be centralised? **(6)**
6. What are the demerits of the line type of organization? **(7)**
7. What are the advantages of the functional (lateral) type of organisation? **(8)**
8. How would you avoid the many disadvantages of the committee type of organisation? **(10)**

CHAPTER III

Environment

1. Introduction. Environment consists of the office building, its furniture and lay-out as well as the physical conditions under which workers operate. This chapter is concerned with the building, lay-out and furniture only.

2. Buying new office premises. The most important factors are:

(*a*) *proximity* to transport, banks, post office, restaurants, markets, customers and staff;

(*b*) *suitability* of floor space for present and anticipated future needs, and the need to conform to s. 5 (2) (overcrowding) of the Offices, Shops and Railway Premises Act 1963;

(*c*) *financial considerations* such as capital outlay and running costs (rates, heating, lighting, insurance, etc.) and possible conversion costs of old buildings;

(*i*) *freehold:* greater capital outlay, permanence of site, freedom to sub-let, greater cost of maintenance;

(*ii*) *leasehold:* smaller capital outlay, risk of rent increase, onerous restrictions on sub-letting, alteration or conversion;

(*d*) *physical factors* such as window space, lifts, heating, lighting, age of building, etc.

3. Out-of-town site, advantages and disadvantages.

(*a*) *Advantages.*

(*i*) Lower building costs.

(*ii*) Less pollution—healthier for employees.

(*iii*) Lower rates and insurance.

(*iv*) Room to expand.

(*b*) *Disadvantages.*

(*i*) Loss of contact with town business associates and customers—some temporary loss of goodwill.

(*ii*) Transport for staff may be difficult.

(*iii*) Absence of shops, restaurants, etc. may render recruitment and retention of staff difficult—women staff in particular like to shop in the lunch hour.

(*iv*) There may still be need for a city office, with the need to install terminals (for electronic data processing).

4. Moving an office. A check list should be prepared as follows.

(*a*) Determine date of the move.

(*b*) Sign contract with the removal company.

(*c*) Appoint a committee and chairman to be responsible for the move.

(*d*) Prepare instructions, appoint employees to assist committee, schedule dates and times, tag and mark all pieces of equipment.

(*e*) Systematically "spring-clean" by destroying accumulated files and papers no longer required.

(*f*) Order cartons and boxes and assign code numbers and put tags on equipment.

(*g*) Issue special instructions about:

(*i*) heavy equipment, such as safes, fireproof files, computer installations—these will be moved before the main date for moving;

(*ii*) desks—these are often placed on end for moving, hence all loose items should be placed in an envelope and transported separately;

(*iii*) office machines—remove bolts holding typewriters, etc. to desks and bring margin stops to the centre of typewriter to prevent the carriage from shifting during the move;

(*iv*) employees' personal property is entirely their responsibility and should be removed by them.

(*h*) Set up direction signs in the new premises.

(*i*) Give clear directions to technicians, electricians, plumbers, etc. about the installations in the new premises. Ensure telephones are ready for immediate use after the move.

(*j*) Check the new premises just prior to the move.

(*k*) Check the new premises just after the move.

5. Location of departments. This refers to the arrangement of many offices within the building. The term *lay-out* is reserved for the arrangement of furniture within a single office.

(*a*) Departments that work together should be adjacent (e.g. the cashier and accountants).

(*b*) Personnel, buying departments, etc., receiving many visitors, should be near the reception area.

(*c*) Locate mail and other service departments centrally.

(*d*) Conference rooms and board room should be at the rear of the building, to be as quiet as possible.

(*e*) Offices using heavy equipment should be on the ground floor.

(*f*) Provide for any later expansion of departments.

(*g*) Allocate private offices only to senior staff (for whom privacy is important).

(*h*) Toilets and cloakrooms should be readily accessible to all staff.

(*i*) Locate drawing offices at the top of the building to obtain maximum light.

(*j*) Provide adequate space for the accumulation of records (not of importance if microfilming is contemplated).

6. The open office. This is one large room where several related departments or sections work together instead of in separate rooms, e.g. personnel and training.

(*a*) *Advantages.*
    (*i*) Better supervision.
    (*ii*) Economy in floor space, lighting, heating, etc.
    (*iii*) Flexibility of lay-out.
    (*iv*) More efficient deployment of machines and equipment.
    (*v*) Minimises movement of staff and documents.

(*b*) *Disadvantages.*
    (*i*) An impersonal atmosphere.
    (*ii*) May look unbusiness-like.
    (*iii*) Communal noise.
    (*iv*) Greater risk of infection from colds, influenza, etc.
    (*v*) Not easy to provide ventilation and heating to everyone's liking.
    (*vi*) Visitors to one section may distract clerks in other sections.

NOTE: An important feature of the open office is the provision for each clerk of a "carrel", similar to the cubicle for readers in a public library.

7. Office landscaping (from Germany, where it is called *Büroland-schaft*). This consists of an open office in which:

(*a*) the furniture is laid out asymmetrically;

(*b*) desks are grouped according to the work function;

(*c*) fitted carpets, flood-lit ceilings, air conditioning, curtained windows and indoor plants between sections combine with the aim of making the office environment as agreeable as possible, and viewed as a total concept.

The asymmetrical lay-out breaks with the traditional rows of desks facing the same direction. Large companies pay the high price of landscaping to improve staff morale and reduce labour turnover.

Its advantages and disadvantages are broadly those stated for and against the open office.

8. Office furniture. Sections 13 and 14 of the Offices, Shops and Railway Premises Act 1963 require "sitting facilities and seats of a design, construction and dimension" suitable for the worker and for the work. Good office furniture saves unnecessary movement of staff, assists supervision and promotes health and efficiency.

9. Factors in buying office furniture.

(a) It should be economical of floor space (note "modular" or "systems" furniture).

(b) It should be functional in relation to the work, e.g. typing.

(c) Height of desk and chair should enable clerk to work without discomfort and without impairing health.

(d) It should be light in weight and easy to move.

(e) It, and the floor on which it stands, should be easy to clean.

(f) Price within the capital budget.

(g) Steel furniture is preferable to wooden furniture (because of fire risk).

10. Office lay-out. This refers to the calculation of space requirements and the detailed use of the total area to provide the best practical arrangement of furniture and equipment. A well-planned office helps:

(a) to increase efficiency of work;

(b) to economise in the use of available floor space; and

(c) to improve and maintain staff morale.

11. Principles of office lay-out.

(a) Simple flow of work, which restricts movement of people and paper. There must not, for example, be any lay-out which permits the "back-tracking" of documents. As far as possible all documents should go forward in a straight line through the office.

(b) Keep the floor space as free as possible from obstruction, serving to promote free passage of employees and to avoid accidents.

(c) Standard floor plan (e.g. desks facing the same way, to the supervisor).

(d) Minimum working space (s. 5 (2) of the Offices, Shops and Railway Premises Act 1963 requires a minimum of 400 cubic feet (11.3 m³) per person). The introduction of word-processing equipment and microprocessors, a notable feature of which is compact bulk, greatly assists more economic use of space, consistent with minimum legal requirements.

(*e*) Sufficient number of gangways, of adequate width.

(*f*) Detailed work needing plenty of light should be sited close to windows.

(*g*) Segregate noisy machines in separate rooms: provide security for expensive installations, e.g. computer terminals.

(*h*) The office should be easy to clean.

(*i*) The office should be easy to evacuate quickly in case of fire, etc.

PROGRESS TEST 3

1. Your directors propose to move the head office from a busy city site to a country site some 10 kilometres away. What are the major factors influencing their choice of site? (**2**)

2. Draw a plan of the personnel department in a company employing 2000 persons, using the following information:

Staff	*Accommodation required*
Personnel manager	Private office
Two or three assistants, with duties divided among them (e.g. employment, training)	One office
Secretarial and clerical staff as required	One office Waiting-room and interview room (**4**)

3. What are the major disadvantages of the open-plan office? (**5**)

4. What is office landscaping and what are its merits? (**6**)

5. Office furniture includes several types of desk. What types are appropriate for:

(*a*) a typist; (*b*) secretary; (*c*) a ledger clerk; (*d*) a calculator; (*e*) a card-punch operator? (**7**)

6. From your own experience suggest three examples of bad office lay-out. (**8**)

CHAPTER IV

Physical Conditions

1. Physical conditions. These are important because:

(a) Health of workers is affected, e.g.
- (i) the effect of bad lighting on sight;
- (ii) excessive noise on nerves;
- (iii) overcrowding on morale;
- (iv) draughts on physical health.

(b) Effect on the efficiency of the office, e.g.
- (i) bad light causes errors;
- (ii) noise, bad heating and ventilation cause distraction.

2. Offices, Shops and Railway Premises Act 1963.

(a) Defines what is an office (rather lengthy).

(b) Exemptions are granted:
- (i) where business is staffed by close relatives, and
- (ii) where weekly hours normally worked do not exceed 21.

(c) The Act requires minimal standards (although they are loosely defined in many cases, such as "sufficient and suitable") in the following aspects:

(i) Cleanliness.	(viii) Washing facilities.
(ii) Prevention of overcrowding.	(ix) Drinking water.
	(x) Accommodation for clothing.
(iii) Temperature.	
(iv) Ventilation.	(xi) Seats for sedentary workers.
(v) Lighting.	
(vi) Sanitary conveniences.	(xii) Eating facilities.
	(xiii) Fencing of machinery.
vii) First aid.	(xiv) Fire precautions.

(d) More precise standards are laid down for the following:

(i) Temperature of 60.8° F (16° C) by one hour after the office opens.

(ii) Minimum of 400 cu. ft. (11.3 m³) of space per worker—ignoring ceiling height above 10 ft. (3 m).

(iii) Every employer with more than 20 employees must obtain a fire certificate from the fire authority (that reasonable precautions have been taken).

(*iv*) Once a week sweeping or cleaning of floors.

(*v*) Every office must have a first aid box, and where there are more than 150 employees at least one person must be trained in first aid.

(*vi*) Sanitary conveniences must be provided: if more than five employees there must be separate ones for each sex, and then 5 for the first 100, and 4 for each 100 employees subsequently.

(*vii*) Wash-basins must be provided in the same ratios to staff as sanitary conveniences.

(*viii*) A supply of drinking water must also be made available.

3. Installations, etc.

(*a*) *Decoration* should be appropriate to each room; cheerful, with maximum reflective power of light.

(*b*) *Noise.* Hard surfaces reflect and soft surfaces absorb noise. External noises are to a great extent uncontrollable, but internal noises should be reduced. Methods of reducing noise include:

(*i*) local absorption, e.g. felt under typewriters;
(*ii*) general absorption, by fitting acoustic ceilings;
(*iii*) segregation of noisy machines;
(*iv*) fitting of carpets;
(*v*) banging doors fitted with door checks.

(*c*) *Lighting* should be of the right quantity and the right quality, and in the right positions. Quality of light is related to type of fitting (direct, indirect, etc.), and the test of good lighting is absence of glare and absence of hard black shadows.

Fluorescent lighting is economical, is nearest to daylight, but capital outlay should be related to price paid per unit of electricity and amount of time in use.

(*d*) *Ventilation.* A constant flow of clean fresh air—without causing draughts. Open windows cause bad feelings, but air-conditioning is not always satisfactory and may be expensive to install.

(*e*) *Heating* involves problems of generating heat and then conserving it. Heating appliances are mostly either of the radiation or the convection type. Convection heating creates a warm current of air and is generally preferred. Heating, mainly by convection, includes:

(*i*) central heating with hot water radiators and pipes;
(*ii*) oil-filled electric radiators;
(*iii*) electric floor-warming;
(*iv*) ducted warm air.

(*f*) *Cleanliness.* Office cleaning should be properly supervised and proper equipment provided, and a timetable should be laid down for more inaccessible places.

(g) *Safety precautions.*

(i) Regular inspection of machines (particularly those electrically operated).

(ii) No trailing telephone wires on floor.

(iii) Ensuring that filing cabinets do not topple over (e.g. by not filling top drawers while the lower ones are empty).

(iv) Ensuring that floors are not too highly polished.

(v) Inspect loose and frayed carpeting that needs repair.

(vi) Provision of steps for reaching high shelves.

(vii) Provision of first aid box.

(viii) Proper siting of electric fires and other portable fires.

(h) *Health and Safety at Work etc. Act 1974.* This Act lays a general duty on every employer to ensure the health, safety and welfare at work of all his employees. The areas covered by this general duty include information and training, the building itself and the working environment. The Act also requires employers of more than five employees to prepare a written statement of their safety policy, and provides for the appointment of safety representatives by recognised trade unions and for the setting up of safety committees. All employees also have a general duty under the Act to take reasonable care for the health and safety of themselves and others.

PROGRESS TEST 4

1. What are the main requirements of the Offices, Shops and Railway Premises Act 1963?   (2)

2. Explain the importance of physical surroundings in offices. (1)

3. Write notes on office lighting, heating and ventilation.   (3)

4. Discuss noise in relation to office work, and ways in which noise can be reduced.   (3)

5. Discuss artificial lighting in relation to office work.   (3)

6. What measures would you take to minimise the risks of personal injury in a general office?   (3)

7. Your advice has been sought on office lighting for a new office block. What points would you stress?   (3)

CHAPTER V

Job Grading and Merit Rating

1. Introduction. Personnel management includes:

    (*a*) recruiting of staff;
    (*b*) their training;
    (*c*) methods of payment;
    (*d*) their promotion;
    (*e*) their dismissal, redundancy and retirement.

It is a difficult aspect in practice because it involves the control and understanding of human beings. It is, therefore, more of an art than a science, although increasing stress is laid upon the relevance of the behavioural sciences, notably industrial psychology.

Much of what is done in personnel management is custom, some is required by law and much of it is rule of thumb, created to suit the occasion.

2. Job grading. This is the scientific assessment of the work content of all jobs in an organisation and their classification into broad categories called *job grades*. The different job grades are then related to different salary scales.

The purpose of job grading has been defined as "a technique for determining the differences between different jobs". This is partly true, for it is really a method of rationalising rates of pay in a business; without it, job grading becomes extremely diverse.

EXAMPLE: (Institute of Administrative Management):

Grade A. Simple tasks under *close supervision*.

Grade B. Simple tasks with work checked, but with a small *measure of responsibility*.

Grade C. More responsible work than B; also checks Grade B work.

Grade D. Work calling for some *initiative*, with little supervision.

Grade E. Work requiring special knowledge and *more responsibility* and working *without supervision*.

Grade F. Supervisory grade, requiring special knowledge, experience, judgment, etc.

Grade G. Tasks requiring professional or specialised knowledge equivalent to a university first degree or to an advanced, but not necessarily final, qualification of a relevant professional association, e.g. ACA, ICSA, etc.

Grade H. Tasks requiring:

(*a*) professional or specialised knowledge equivalent to a university first degree, with some experience, or a final qualification of the associations noted in Grade G;

(*b*) an extensive measure of expertise and judgment in work of significant complexity or importance;

(*c*) supervision of a range normally of 20 or more clerical staff.

3. Techniques of job grading. There are several techniques, but the most usual one is the pointing method.

(*a*) Evaluate all jobs and draw up *job specifications* (detailed descriptions of work content) for every job.

(*b*) Draw up a list of all the qualities inherent in every job, and give them a weighted number of points, e.g.:

(*i*) *Experience* up to 20 points.

(*ii*) *Education* up to 12 points.

(*iii*) *Complexity* up to 10 points.

(*iv*) *Responsibility* for production of information, or for the care of cash, up to 12 points.

(*v*) *Supervision* (of others) up to 10 points.

(*vi*) *Initiative* up to 10 points.

(*c*) In the light of these qualities, award every job its quota of points under each heading.

(*d*) Draft a scale of point values for each job grade (it is usual to have between six and ten job grades), e.g.:

(*i*) Grade 1:61 points and over.

(*ii*) Grade 2:50 to 60 points.

(*iii*) Grade 3:40 to 49 points.

(*iv*) Grade 4:20 to 39 points.

(*v*) Grade 5:10 to 19 points.

(*vi*) Grade 6:Under 10 points.

(*e*) Different salary scales are then allotted to each job grade.

4. Advantages and disadvantages of job grading.

(*a*) *Advantages*.

(*i*) Ensures that staff doing the same kind of work receive the same rates of pay, thus avoiding wage anomalies.

(*ii*) Assists in evaluating new jobs and deciding on appropriate rates of pay.

(*iii*) Helps in selecting new staff; no bargaining over salaries.

(*iv*) Assists in drafting training schemes and promotion requirements from one grade to another.

(*v*) Assists in transferring employees from one department to another.

(*vi*) Useful in cost estimating and budgetary control.

(*b*) *Disadvantages*.

(*i*) Failure to evaluate periodically (the work content of the same job varies from time to time).

(*ii*) By itself, job grading fails to take account of individual differences in ability.

(*iii*) Tendency to view the worker (instead of the work content) as the grade.

(*iv*) Assessment of job grading is not purely scientific, and may be subjective only.

(*v*) It places all jobs into a few grades and reduces chances of promotion.

5. Job grading and clerical work. It is difficult to apply job grading to clerical work successfully, for in addition to the above-mentioned difficulties:

(*a*) it is very difficult to measure clerical work in the job evaluation;

(*b*) clerical work is subject to many interruptions (telephone calls, settling of queries, etc.);

(*c*) imponderable qualities like loyalty and initiative are interpreted in different ways by different people;

(*d*) assessment may not be on the same basis throughout the organisation because of the different work content of different jobs.

6. Merit rating (staff reporting, or staff appraisal). This is the regular periodic assessment of how well a worker is doing his job. It is subjective and its purpose is to assess ability for the purposes of promotion, and/or to award extra pay for extra effort.

The basic qualities usually assessed are:

(*a*) quality of work performed;
(*b*) quantity of work performed;
(*c*) co-operativeness (or loyalty);
(*d*) dependability (related to the degree of supervision required).

Merit rating of every employee up to supervisory level is usually carried out once a year.

It should, in the first instance, be completed by an employee's immediate superior: he is the only one who can really assess the ability of an employee. In an attempt to overcome bias, it is sometimes assessed by a joint committee of executives, e.g. consisting of the man's supervisor, the company secretary, and the personnel officer.

7. Merit rating publication. Should employees be told of their ratings?

(a) *In favour*.

(i) Employees have a right to know of their progress.

(ii) Secret reports are bad for morale.

(iii) Employees should know where they have to improve themselves.

(b) *Against*.

(i) It may lead to arguments with employees.

(ii) Merit rating is intended only to assist management.

(iii) It may dishearten the average employee.

(c) *Compromise*.

(i) Notify employees only if the rating is unfavourable to them, i.e. worse than before.

(ii) No recording of anything which is unsatisfactory.

8. Advantages and disadvantages of merit rating.

(a) *Advantages*.

(i) Gives recognition to workers of greater ability.

(ii) Compensates for some of the disadvantages of job grading.

(iii) Useful to employees to know of their standing (if published for them).

(iv) Fairest method of promotion (normal ratings are made regardless of impending vacancies).

(v) Supervisors are encouraged to judge consistently, and to put their judgments in writing.

(vi) It is a stimulus to workers to make greater effort when they know that merit rating is taking place.

(b) *Disadvantages*.

(i) Does not prevent favouritism.

(ii) Not usually done often enough to be a fair assessment.

(iii) No way of proving validity of rating (except by transfer of employees from one department to another).

(iv) There is no precise scientific method of measuring "merit".

(v) Supervisors often need training in the technique of merit rating (e.g. too many "average" markings).

(vi) Qualities may be too imponderable to assess.

(*vii*) If not published, it fails as an incentive to employees.

(*viii*) If merit ratings are not made more frequently than once a year, they may be coloured by recent happenings.

9. Institute of Administrative Management merit grades for clerical work. Inside each job grade there should be merit ratings for the following classes of employee:

Merit grade 1. Starter
            2. Qualified
            3. Experienced
            4. Superior
            5. Outstanding

PROGRESS TEST 5

1. Ought a personnel officer to be instructed in the principles of Industrial Psychology? (**1**)

2. What is the basic difference between job grading and merit rating? (**2, 6**)

3. Describe the pointing method of job grading. (**3**)

4. How seriously do you view, as a disadvantage of job grading, the tendency to view the worker rather than the job content? (**4**)

5. What kinds of clerical work are more suitable than others for job grading? (**5**)

6. What is staff appraisal and by whom should it be done? (**6**)

7. Argue the case for and against publication of merit ratings. (**7**)

8. Describe the Administrative Management merit rating scheme for office workers. (**9**)

CHAPTER VI

Salary Scales and Welfare

1. Advantages of having salary scales.

(*a*) Employees know that they are being paid the rate for the job.

(*b*) They know the rates of pay for the higher grades and can assess their promotion prospects.

(*c*) Secrecy with regard to salaries (which is harmful to morale) is eliminated.

(*d*) The suspicion that salary increases are made arbitrarily is removed.

2. Major factors in drafting salary scales.

(*a*) Define different scales for different categories of work.

(*b*) Salaries should preferably be above the market rate, but should not be uneconomically high: regard must be had to the salary budget.

(*c*) The scales should reflect the importance of experience in a job.

(*d*) Define maximum and minimum rates to give flexibility.

(*e*) Have the right number of intermediate increments: too many at short intervals causes impatience and too few at long intervals leads to frustration.

(*f*) Provide for deferred increments when workers have been on maximum rates for years.

(*g*) The Equal Pay Act 1970 requires that male and female staff must be paid the same rate when they are doing the same or broadly similar work or work rated as equivalent under job evaluation.

(*h*) Offer payment according to age for juniors. Maximum age is a policy decision.

(*i*) Consider some aspect of "cost of living" increases and "London allowances", etc. when fixing scales.

(*j*) Salary scales should be simple and easy to understand and operate.

3. High salary as incentive to high productivity. Economic theory

teaches that "high wages are cheap wages; low wages are dear wages", and if high salaries are offered to attract the best employees available, high productivity is expected to follow. However, once a clerk has settled down, the relative size of his salary scale is soon forgotten and hence, in practice, a company must offer additional incentives such as:

(*a*) good management (especially fair supervision);
(*b*) good working conditions;
(*c*) good welfare facilities;
(*d*) joint consultation;
(*e*) co-partnership and profit-sharing schemes;
(*f*) proper promotion policy and opportunities for training;
(*g*) good human relations.

4. Welfare. This is any service or amenity provided by an employer in addition to normal wages and salaries. Most large companies provide generous welfare facilities in the knowledge that staff morale is thereby improved and maintained: smaller companies may have to offer higher salaries to compensate for the lack of the sophisticated welfare which they cannot provide. Welfare can be analysed as follows:

(*a*) *Legal welfare:* that required by the State under the various Factory Acts and under the Offices, Shops and Railway Premises Act 1963, e.g. "suitable and sufficient eating facilities" (s. 15). Superannuation is provided under the Social Security Pensions Act 1975.

(*b*) *Economic welfare:*
  (*i*) profit-sharing (the annual "bonus");
  (*ii*) loans to buy houses and cars;
  (*iii*) provision of transport to and from work.

(*c*) *Humanitarian or social welfare:*
  (*i*) medical services beyond those required by Act of Parliament;
  (*ii*) subsidised meals in the company canteen or refectory;
  (*iii*) luncheon vouchers to be spent by employees at local restaurants;
  (*iv*) sport, drama and other "social club" activities, which are normally organised by the employees themselves, the company subsidising at least the capital expenditure.

By improving the morale of employees, welfare plays an important role in recruitment, in improving productivity and reducing labour turnover.

5. Staff handbook. This is a booklet issued to new employees (usually on induction) to help them understand the company and to quicken their interest in it. The usual contents are:

(*a*) the history, products and organisation of the company;

(*b*) conditions of service, holidays, sick pay, hours of duty, including flexitime (if any), overtime payments, superannuation, etc.;

(*c*) welfare facilities, protective clothing, sports clubs, safety measures, joint consultation, etc.;

(*d*) trade union membership;

(*e*) company regulations about personal hygiene and dress, right of search, etc.

PROGRESS TEST 6

1. Maximum and minimum rates are usually stated in salary scales. Why is it important to do so? **(2)**

2. State five major factors in drafting salary scales. **(2)**

3. Examine the contention that a high salary is the only realistic incentive to high productivity. **(3)**

4. What are the economic aspects of welfare? **(4)**

5. What is the importance of welfare? **(4)**

6. State what you consider to be the *minimum* contents of a staff handbook. **(5)**

CHAPTER VII

Recruitment of Staff

1. Sources of clerical staff of all grades.

(*a*) Advertising in national and local newspapers, trade and professional journals.

(*b*) Employment Service Division employment office or job-centre (for unskilled clerical labour).

(*c*) Employment Service Division Professional and Executive Register (for management staff).

(*d*) Private employment agencies which perform initial screening. This is the best way to obtain a replacement in an emergency.

(*e*) Ex-employees whose record is good.

(*f*) Recommendations from existing employees, although the charge of nepotism is easily levelled in such cases and less easily refuted in practice.

(*g*) Office appliance companies (notably those dealing with computers) where machines and equipment are purchased: operators trained by them come with the appliances.

(*h*) Hospitals and ex-service organisations.

(*i*) Professional organisations (which maintain an employment register).

(*j*) Schools, colleges and universities, for juniors or for graduates.

(*k*) Careers officers in schools assume increasing importance in view of the difficulties facing young people in finding employment. It is important that these officers be properly trained in industrial problems affecting the employment of young people.

(*l*) By internal promotion from existing staff.

2. Management selection agencies. These undertake the advertising and initial screening, then submit short lists to employers.

(*a*) *Advantages.*
  (*i*) impartiality;
  (*ii*) specialised interviewing techniques.
(*b*) *Disadvantages.*

(i) do not know thoroughly the business for which the applicant is required;

(ii) charge high fees.

Note also the Government-sponsored scheme for retired officers from the Services. A senior retired officer is appointed to direct and sponsor officers to suitable executive positions in industry. Their appointment follows a re-orientation course at a Polytechnic or College of Further Education.

3. Level of entry. Many large companies have a two-level entry of junior clerks.

(a) *Age 16*, with appropriate "O" levels or the equivalent CSE. English and mathematics are usually essential. Successful applicants will be employed as general clerks.

(b) *Age 18*, with appropriate "A" levels and supporting "O" levels, again with emphasis on English and mathematics. Successful applicants will become commercial trainees.

4. Basic procedure on application. All applicants for clerical positions will comply with the following basic procedure.

(a) Send an application form to the personnel officer. This will normally require a short letter from the candidate in addition to his/her personal details.

(b) An applicant whom the personnel officer has placed on the "short list" will be asked to attend for interview.

(c) Tests, such as the J. R. Morrisby "test battery profile" and the various literacy and numeracy tests devised by the National Institute of Industrial Psychology will be given to the candidates. Most personnel officers prefer to set the tests before the interview. The Cattell 16 PF test is widely used.

(d) The candidates attend an interview.

(e) References are taken up either before or after the interview.

(f) Successful candidates will be informed by letter of the fact of the contract of employment, its terms and conditions, and of the starting date and time.

5. The interview. Few functions of the personnel officer are as important as interviewing candidates for employment as clerks. A good clerk brings to his job much more than literacy and numeracy. An employer offering not less than the market tate of salary and prospects, is entitled to require also integrity, loyalty and willingness to co-operate with colleagues. The basic purposes of the interview are, therefore:

(*a*) to assess character and personality;

(*b*) to fill in gaps in application forms;

(*c*) to assess the candidate's ability to perform the relevant duties;

(*d*) to inform the candidate further about the job;

(*e*) to make a contract of employment.

The seven-point plan devised by the National Institute of Industrial Psychology is widely used by many interviewers, who have with them at the interview a form similar to that outlined in Table II, i.e. a list of attributes required in a successful applicant for a required job.

TABLE II: Seven-point plan for interviewing staff.

Characteristic	Essential	Desirable
Physique		
Attainments		
General intelligence		
Special aptitudes		
Interests		
Disposition		
Circumstances		

6. Interviewing arrangements. It is important to remember that an interview is a two-way process: the applicant interviews the prospective employer as well as being interviewed by him. It is, therefore, essential to do nothing to impair the company's image in the eyes of applicants, although in the rare case of the stress interview, sometimes applied to applicants for senior positions, the interviewer sets out deliberately to challenge, and even provoke, the applicant to test his ability to maintain an even temper. The basic arrangements are:

(*a*) ensure that the letter calling the applicant to interview states clearly the three unities of time, place and action;

(*b*) arrange the furniture to give a friendly, informal and private impression;

(*c*) match the job specification with the application;

(*d*) arrange interviews at intervals (not all at the same time).

7. References and testimonials.

(*a*) Testimonials are usually general in character, addressed "To whom it may concern".

(*b*) References are normally addressed by one employer to another.

References and testimonials are rarely sufficient by themselves in determining a person's eligibility for a position. They may often be misleading: e.g. an employer writing a reference for a clerk still in his employment may "damn him with faint praise" because he does not want to lose him: conversely, a reference full of praise for the employee is often interpreted to imply that the writer wishes to be rid of him.

8. Legal aspects of references and testimonials. An ex-employer is under no legal obligation to furnish a reference concerning an ex-employee, but if he chooses to do so at the request of the employee, or, more usually, of the prospective employer, he is liable in the tort of libel to the employee if he defames him by using words which expose him to ridicule, hatred or contempt of all right-thinking people, causing him to be shunned and avoided. If, however, the letter is a privileged communication, any legal action by the employee will fail. A privileged communication is one which:

(*a*) the writer has a social, legal or moral duty to write and there is on the part of the addressee a corresponding social, legal or moral interest in reading it;

(*b*) was not "unduly published", i.e. the writer took all reasonable steps, e.g. by marking the envelope "private and confidential", to ensure that the reference was read only by the prospective employer;

(*c*) was not inspired by malice, i.e. the ex-employer did not abuse the defence of qualified privilege to gratify some private grudge or spite against the employee.

The ex-employer may also be liable to a new employer if he fails to inform him that, e.g. the employee is a convicted thief, and the new employer engages him to his own detriment.

9. Service agreements. The contents of a service agreement would be as follows:

(*a*) *For an agreement with a manager:*

(*i*) Rate or remuneration. Clauses would be necessary to cover expense allowance, commission on profits or sales and probably a car allowance (or provision of a car).

(*ii*) Duties would normally be specified (though this is not required by law), but for a manager the wording would be non-specific, e.g. for a general manager, "to perform such duties as directed by the board of directors from time to time".

(b) *For an apprentice* there might be special clauses:

(i) Employee must not make use of "trade secrets".

(ii) Clause binding the employee for a certain number of years.

(iii) Prevention, after termination of employment, from carrying on a similar trade or profession within a certain geographical area.

(c) In addition, for all important service agreements, there would be a clause dealing with the method of *arbitration* in case of dispute.

10. Employment Protection (Consolidation) Act 1978. The Act requires a statement in writing (not quite the same as a contract) to be given to *all* employees within thirteen weeks of their engagement. Requirements of the Act on such statements:

(a) identification of the parties;

(b) date of commencement of employment;

(c) rate of remuneration and method of calculation;

(d) intervals at which it is to be paid;

(e) terms and conditions of service relating to hours of work;

(f) terms, etc. relating to holidays and holiday pay;

(g) terms, etc. relating to sickness and sick pay;

(h) terms, etc. relating to pensions and pension schemes;

(i) length of notice to be given by either side;

(j) entitlement to holidays including public holidays, and so that holiday pay entitlement can be calculated on termination of employment i.e. if any remains to the employee;

(k) right to belong to a registered trade union;

(l) right not to belong to a union;

(m) the person with whom one should take up a grievance, and the stages in the subsequent grievance procedure;

(n) job title;

(o) disciplinary rules and method of appeal against discipline.

11. Other legislation affecting employment. The major Acts are:

(a) The Equal Pay Act 1970;

(b) The Sex Discrimination Act 1975;

(c) The Employment Protection Act 1975;

(d) The Race Relations Act 1976;

(e) Employment Act 1980.

This flood of recent legislation relating to employment greatly increases the complexity of office administration. Some of it is dominated by political philosophy and changes are likely as governments change. Students of this aspect of office administration must necessarily keep up-to-date by consulting any amending or new legislation. A wide range of explanatory booklets may be obtained free of charge at the local Department of Employment, e.g. the very detailed guide to the Race Relations Act 1976.

12. Long term planning. A large company cannot live hand-to-mouth by replacing staff one by one as vacancies occur. Hence a policy of annual intake of junior clerks must be related to the future needs of the organisation.

EXAMPLE:

The organisation of a large company requires among its total clerical staff 30 highly trained clerks capable of assuming responsibility, including supervision. During a six-year cycle, observed from the personnel department's records, there is much wastage, caused mainly by the promotion of exceptionally competent clerks to higher levels.

The statistics are as shown in Table III.

TABLE III: Turnover of staff.

Year	% of fully trained special staff remaining
0	100
1	90
2	50
3	30
4	20
5	10
6	0
Total	300

If an annual intake of 100 persons yields a total work force of 300, then the annual intake necessary to attain, and maintain, a constant strength of 30 persons is:

$$\frac{100}{300} \times 30 = 10$$

The staffing and recruitment schedule for the specified group is, accordingly, as in Table IV.

TABLE IV: Staffing and Recruitment Schedule

Factors:	1.0	0.9	0.5	0.3	0.2	0.1		
Years:	0	1	2	3	4	5	6	etc.
Employees:	30	27	15	9	6	3	0	0
	10	9	5	3	2	1	0	0
		10	9	5	3	2	1	0
			10	9	5	3	2	1
				10	9	5	3	2
					10	9	5	3
						10	9	5
							10	9
								10 etc.
Totals:	40	46	39	36	35	33	30	30

It will be observed that the steady state—the required special staff of 30 persons—is attained at the sixth year, although in the first five years of the existence of the office, when training needs are more urgent than when the organisation has stabilised, the company employs more than the required final minimum of 30.

This example is over-simplified and begs many questions, but it does emphasise the urgent need to plan staff recruitment for a large office with reference both to immediate, and long-term requirements.

PROGRESS TEST 7

1. How would you replace a senior clerk in an emergency? (1)
2. Describe a test frequently given to applicants for junior clerical appointments. (4)
3. What qualities and attainments do you look for when engaging an applicant for junior general clerical duties? (5)
4. What is the seven-point plan? (5)
5. An interview is a two-way process. Explain the importance of this concept. (6)
6. John Smith was employed by you as a sales ledger clerk for two years. During that time his work was satisfactory, but small sums of money were occasionally missing, although no proof of

his responsibility was ever forthcoming. Since he left, no further losses have been reported. The personnel officer of Squaredealers Ltd, to whom Smith has applied for the post of sales ledger clerk, has asked you for a reference. Draft a suitable letter. **(7)**

7. What is a privileged communication? **(8)**

8. What special clauses should appear in the service agreement of: (*a*) a manager; (*b*) an apprentice? **(9)**

9. What must be given to all employees within thirteen weeks of their engagement? **(10)**

10. Why is long-term planning essential in recruitment of staff? **(12)**

CHAPTER VIII

Induction, Training and Promotion of Staff

1. Induction. The induction of new employees is an aspect of employment procedure which is increasingly recognised as essential to the two-sided process whereby, on the employer's part, the new employee has to be turned into a worker deriving satisfaction from his work, friendship with his colleagues and pride in belonging to a company with local and national prestige, and, on his part, the new employee wants to ask many questions, and doubts and fears often worry him.

In a large company, with fully qualified personnel staff, induction will be organised to last for several days before the new employees of the annual intake actually commence work. The induction process includes:

(*a*) a tour of the offices and factories;

(*b*) talks and films showing the history of the company, the products and where they are sold;

(*c*) explanations of company policy relating to holidays, sickness, promotion, trade union membership, etc.;

(*d*) job description, as a preliminary to subsequent job training.

2. Training. The major levels of training include the following.

(*a*) *Induction training.* This aims at settling the new employee in the job for which he has been engaged.

(*b*) *Job training.* This is specialised instruction on how to do a specific job.

(*c*) *Supervisory training* aims at teaching employees the skills of supervision, control and training of others.

(*d*) *Management training.* This seeks to enable suitable employees to qualify for the higher levels of company organisation, e.g. company secretary or registrar, accountant, etc.

(*e*) *Executive development.* To develop the abilities of the company's executives.

Advice on all levels of training can be obtained from the Industrial Training Boards established under the Industrial Training Act 1964.

3. The importance of training.

(*a*) Contributes to employee morale.

(*b*) The trainee learns early by his own mistakes and the job will be more efficiently performed.

(*c*) It ensures continuity of candidates for higher levels of employment.

(*d*) Trainees learn the standard methods.

(*e*) Helps to reduce staff turnover.

4. Methods of training.

(*a*) *Induction training* (described in **1**).

(*b*) *Job training*.

(*i*) By a system of understudies to experienced workers. This is not generally to be recommended; the old hands may be reluctant, or unable adequately, to train new employees.

(*ii*) In internal company schools, where exact working conditions can be simulated.

(*iii*) At skillcentres (courses run by the Training Services Division of the Manpower Services Commission), or by part-time day release at Colleges of Further Education and Polytechnics to qualify for National or Higher National Certificates in Business Studies, or for professional accountancy and secretarial qualifications.

(*iv*) Commercial trainees, normally aged over 18, with "A" Level qualifications, in addition to day release to college, spend several months working in each of the company's departments, including, for example, the administration of the company's shop selling food, etc., to employees.

(*c*) *Supervisory training*.

(*i*) Training within industry (TWI) course of the Training Services Division. A typical course for prospective supervisors is organised by the training department of the company. It lasts from six to seven days during which time a group of not more than a dozen employees attends lectures on job instruction, job relations, disciplinary action, departmental induction, basic arithmetic, etc.

(*ii*) Office supervisors' course by part-time day release or evening study for, e.g. the office supervisors' certificate of the Institute of Administrative Management.

(*d*) *Management training and executive development*.

(*i*) By part-time day release to qualify for, e.g. the Diploma in Management Studies.

(*ii*) By granting a year's leave from the office to study full-time for the Diploma in Management Studies, or two terms per year for each of three years to qualify for the Higher National Diploma (Sandwich) in Business Studies.

(*iii*) By attendance of suitable employees at short, intensive courses in management, marketing, etc., at Regional Management Centres.

(*iv*) By flying squad method of rotation of management trainees within the various departments of the organisation.

5. The difficulties of training.

(*a*) Cost—the training officer in practice has to work to a tight budget.

(*b*) Training consumes time of both new and existing employees.

(*c*) Training may dislocate work.

(*d*) Experienced and professionally qualified training officers are not easy to obtain.

(*e*) Standard methods are not always applicable to company practice.

6. Clerical training technique.

(*a*) Draft a syllabus.

(*b*) Explain the purpose of the training, the relationship of the subject-matter with other work and the relative importance of details and the manner of performance.

(*c*) Start with known things and lead on to the unknown.

(*d*) Explain simple things before the complicated: always speak to the condition of the trainees.

(*e*) Make full use of overhead projectors, films, practical demonstrations, etc.

(*f*) Give reasons for each operation.

(*g*) Go slowly: speed is a habit which comes later.

(*h*) As soon as possible involve the trainee by letting him/her try his/her hand.

(*i*) Comment on the performance and repeat if necessary.

(*j*) Follow up at frequent intervals to test competence.

(*k*) Remember above all that "men should be taught as if you taught them not, and things unknown proposed as things forgot".

7. Preparing a training programme.

(*a*) Classify the types of training needed and the numbers of new employees expected for each.

(*b*) Consider the methods to be applied, estimate their financial cost and whether the budget will permit them.

(c) Estimate the time to be spent by existing employees in helping with the training.

(d) Always train the right number: if too many are trained, dissatisfaction will be caused when promotions go to only a few, and labour turnover will increase.

(e) Give publicity, via notice boards, house magazines, etc., of training facilities available, e.g. it may be useful to permit existing staff to join in part of training for new employees.

(f) Commence keeping control records of trainees' names, examination results, etc.

8. Promotion and transfers. A carefully drafted procedure is essential for:

(a) a transfer of an employee from one job to another; this is as important as placement and training of new employees;

(b) a promotion from within the organisation;

(c) a promotion from outside the company.

9. Promotion from outside.

(a) Advantages.

(i) There is a wider field of selection normally available and abler candidates may be available.

(ii) The candidates will bring fresh minds, a wider experience, and, possibly a broader outlook.

(b) Disadvantages.

(i) They will require more formal and informal training than internal candidates.

(ii) They may take a long time to settle down.

(iii) Their employment refutes the company's alleged interest in its established employees and there may be considerable resentment against the newcomer and the company alike.

10. The criteria for promotion.

(a) *Ability* (not easy to assess). Its advantages are:

(i) it is best for efficiency of work;

(ii) it is fairest to workers, provoking least resentment;

(iii) it conduces both to greater efficiency and keenness among the staff by introducing an element of competitiveness into an office.

It is to be noted, however, that ability in a particular job does not, of itself, imply ability at a higher level.

(b) *Seniority* (waiting for "dead men's shoes"). Its advantages are:

(*i*) it gives reward for long service;

(*ii*) it recognises the worth of experience;

(*iii*) it helps the morale of staff.

It is to be noted that, notwithstanding the importance of ability and seniority as criteria, the imponderable qualities of loyalty and reliability are highly regarded by many employers.

(*c*) *The results of an examination*; widely used in the Civil Service.

(*d*) *By personal interview*; qualities of leadership may have developed quickly since first employment.

(*e*) *By arbitrary selection* conditioned by personal likes and dislikes.

(*f*) *By some combination* of any of the foregoing.

11. Staff records. These are essential as an index of staff when reviewing transfers, promotions or disciplinary action. They normally contain the history of employees in the business, showing departments worked in, salary scales, family data, black marks such as bad time-keeping, etc. The major forms of staff record are:

(*a*) visible card index;

(*b*) folder system (one for each employee);

(*c*) a combined application form and staff record in the form of an individual envelope for each employee;

(*d*) microfilm;

(*e*) punched card, or magnetic tape.

Note that it is possible to duplicate records in this, and many other contexts, e.g. the wages department will have many relevant details concerning staff.

Note also the usefulness of the house magazine in reporting employees' activities in the company's social and sporting amenities: unsuspected qualities of enterprise and leadership may thereby be highlighted.

PROGRESS TEST 8

1. Why is a thorough induction course necessary?   (**1**)

2. Assess the importance of training.   (**3**)

3. State the major methods of training of clerks.   (**4**)

4. What provision is normally made for management training? (**4**)

5. What help in training is afforded by Colleges of Further Education and Polytechnics?   (**4**)

6. What are the basic difficulties of training?   (**5**)

7. State the major techniques of clerical training. **(6)**

8. Why is it important to train the right number of persons? **(7)**

9. What are the disadvantages of: (*a*) promotion by ability; (*b*) promotion by examination; (*c*) promotion by seniority? **(10)**

10. Draft a visible card index to record staff data. **(11)**

CHAPTER IX

Flexible Working Hours, Timekeeping and Overtime

1. Flexible working hours. The system originated in Germany in 1965 (where it is called *Gleitzeit*—gliding-time), and has spread rapidly throughout Europe. The essential aim of the system is to allow the employee a limited choice in deciding his starting and finishing times at work each day. This is achieved by dividing his working day into separate periods of "core-time", during which the employee must be at work, and "flexible time", or "flexi-time", during which he may be at work or not, as he chooses.

(a) *Core time.* The core-time varies from company to company, but for office workers, 10 a.m. to 4 p.m. is typical.

(b) *Flexi-time.* The corresponding flexible hours are usually 8 a.m. to 10 a.m. and 4 p.m. to 6 p.m.

(c) *Lunch.* The lunch break is usually taken during the core-time, and this may either be staggered or made of variable length.

(d) *Credits and debits.* The system includes an additional element of flexibility by permitting employees to carry a credit or debit of a few hours over from one accounting period to the next. The employee can build up a credit balance of hours over a period and spend them by taking time off in subsequent flexible periods.

(e) *Time recording.* Strict time-recording is clearly essential if the working hours of each employee are not to get confused and full advantage is to be taken of the scheme. The German MBB scheme requires time cards to be kept for clocking-in by each employee.

(f) *Calculations.* The cards are passed to the computer section at the end of each 10-day period, when a running total of hours is calculated. A final check is made at the end of each month, when special factors such as holidays, overtime and sickness are allowed for.

(g) *Overtime.* Overtime working is outside the flexible scheme: it has to be agreed in advance. Companies may stipulate that, before overtime is worked, the employee must have worked a certain minimum number of hours on the relevant day. Within the limits of the scheme, the employee can choose between getting paid for any overtime and taking time off in lieu during what remains of the accounting period.

2. Merits and demerits of flexible hours.

   (*a*) *Advantages to the employee.*

   (*i*) Accommodating work to the employee's individual rhythms of sleep, concentration and interest.

   (*ii*) Spreading travelling times, thereby avoiding peak periods.

   (*iii*) Dovetailing work and leisure in a more satisfactory way for the individual.

   (*b*) *Advantages to the company.*

   (*i*) Less overtime tends to be worked as employees themselves iron out fluctuations in their work-load.

   (*ii*) Communications improve because supervisors must give clear instructions to cover their own flexible hours.

   (*iii*) Flexible periods are usually quieter than core-time.

   (*iv*) Work previously left over until the next day tends to be finished.

   (*v*) Credit hours rather than debit hours tend to be built up in practice.

   (*vi*) Fewer days are lost through illness and absenteeism.

   (*vii*) There is a significant increase in productivity.

   (*viii*) Employees feel a sense of responsibility.

   (*c*) *Disadvantages to the employer.*

   (*i*) Cost of installing and maintaining the system.

   (*ii*) The normal working day is increased in length, with additional costs of heating, lighting, etc.

   (*iii*) Some reduction in staff coverage during the flexible periods.

   (*d*) *Disadvantages to the employees.*

   (*i*) Loss of overtime pay.

   (*ii*) Loss of dignity because of clocking in and out.

   (*iii*) Supervisors may have to work longer hours.

   (*iv*) Where jobs are related, late arrival of one person may delay others.

3. Methods of time recording.
There are various methods of time recording, both manual and automatic, and the major ones are detailed in the subsequent sections.

4. Time-book.
This is a relatively old-fashioned method suitable for office staff. Employees sign their names and times of arrival and departure. Signatures after a red line is drawn by the super-

visor in the book denote lateness or arrival and delay after departure time. The method is open to fraud and lacks accuracy.

5. Autographer recorder. The employee depresses a lever on the machine, signs his name on a roll of paper and releases the lever. The time is recorded against his signature and the paper roll moves in readiness for the next signature.

(*a*) *Advantages.*

(*i*) Recording of time is automatic and accurate.

(*ii*) Employees cannot alter the record since the roll is locked in the machine.

(*b*) *Disadvantages.*

(*i*) Names appear in random order rather than pay-roll order.

(*ii*) Suitable only for a small staff of a few dozen; no quicker than a time-book.

6. Dial recorder. Names with accompanying pay-roll numbers are written in required order on a large roll of paper which is then locked inside the recorder, on the face of which there is a clock and a large dial bearing numbers in sequence. Employees turn the dial to their pay-roll numbers and depress a lever. The arrival times are thereby automatically recorded against name and number.

(*a*) *Advantages.*

(*i*) Recording is in strict pay-roll order.

(*ii*) An efficient machine has a strong psychological effect in promoting good time-keeping.

(*iii*) It is suitable for factories where dirty work is performed, and where there may be illiterate employees.

(*b*) *Disadvantages.*

(*i*) Employees can easily clock on or off for other employees, either purposely or accidentally. It should be company policy widely to publicise that deliberate use of the recorder for another employee is ground for dismissal without notice.

(*ii*) It is suitable only where employees have one job only—it does not provide media for further wage calculations.

7. Time card recorder. The employee on arrival takes his clock-card bearing his name and number from the OUT rack, puts it in the machine which records the time, and places it in the IN rack. When he leaves, his card, on completion of clocking out, is placed once more in the OUT rack. Normal times are printed in black: lateness and overtime in red.

(a) *Advantages.*

(i) An individual time record is created for each employee.

(ii) Absentees can be checked by a glance at the OUT rack shortly after starting time.

(iii) The time card (or clock card) can be used as authority to receive, and as a receipt for, wages.

(iv) The card can be used for making wage calculations. A rubber stamp, such as shown in Fig. 2, is placed on the back of the

Week ending.		
Flat hours wkd.		
O/time " "		
Production bonus		
Time-keeping bonus		
Total wage	£	

FIG. 2 *Rubber stamp for back of clock cards.*

"clock-cards". Following completion of the pay-roll, the cards may, under some systems, be returned to the employees for checking by them. Wages are handed to employees in exchange for the clock-cards.

(v) The cards may also be ruled to provide additional data for costing purposes.

(b) *Disadvantages.*

(i) In common with dial time-recording, the method can be abused by clocking on or off for other employees.

(ii) Cards can be lost, mislaid or forged.

(iii) Cards are expensive and the system requires strict control.

8. Electronic clocks. These are particularly appropriate for recording flexible working hours, e.g. the ENWH (employee-nominated working hours) recording system, called Selectatime, which consists of a time totalising meter coupled to a key-controlled on/off switch operated by the employee.

9. Overtime. In small companies a flexible policy is usually followed, whereby unpaid overtime is expected, in return for which leave of absence is granted when needed. In addition, tea is normally provided by the employer. There is an increasing tendency, however, for clerical overtime to be paid for on the same basis as that in the factory. A certain amount of overtime is inevitable for, e.g. stocktaking, annual accounts, annual return, dividend payments, etc., but much can be avoided by drawing on staff in other departments who are temporarily available to help.

Badly planned and excessive overtime will affect the health and morale of the staff and increase the rate of labour turnover.

PROGRESS TEST 9

1. "Flexible working hour schemes have something in common with banks." Explain. (**1**)

2. In a certain company operating flexible hours, overtime commences officially at 6 p.m. and is paid for. How would you organise the system to prevent employees from earning too much overtime pay? How would you deal with a situation in which the majority of employees work their flexible hours before the core time? (**1**)

3. What are the advantages of flexible working hours: (*a*) for the employer; (*b*) for the employee? (**2**)

4. On what grounds might employees resist the proposal to introduce flexible working hours? (**2**)

5. Examine the advantages and disadvantages of the use of time-books. (**4**)

6. What steps would you take to minimise the disadvantages of time-card recorders? (**7**)

7. Discuss the usefulness of clock-cards. (**7**)

8. Draft a "pie" diagram to illustrate a typical "flexi-time" programme for an office. (**1**)

CHAPTER X

Dismissal of Staff, Labour Turnover and Morale

1. Current legislation (July 1983). The Employment Protection (Consolidation) Act 1978, which came into force on 1 November 1978 brought together in one enactment the provisions on employment previously contained in The Redundancy Payments Act 1965, The Contracts of Employment Act 1972, The Trade Union and Labour Relations Acts 1974 & 1976 and The Employment Protection Act 1975.

The Employment Act 1980 made a number of important amendments to The Trade Union and Labour Relations Acts 1974 & 1976, The Employment Protection Act 1975, and The Employment Protection (Consolidation) Act 1978.

The Employment Act 1982 made important changes in all of the above legislation.

Students are urged to consult the Department of Employment's compendium of booklets (Students' Edition) on current employment legislation.

2. The Contract of employment. The Employment Protection (Consolidation) Act 1978 requires an employer within 13 weeks of commencement of employment to give to every employee a written statement about the main terms of employment with an additional note on disciplinary and grievance procedures (*see* Chapter VII, **10**, for the details of the statement). The statement can be used as important evidence of terms and conditions of an unwritten contract.

An employer who re-engages on the same terms an employee whose period of employment ended within the last six months need not give him or her another written contract.

3. Dismissal. The Employment Protection (Consolidation) Act 1978, (amended by the Employment Act 1980) gives, to most employees, the right not to be unfairly dismissed.

Dismissal can be "fair" only if the employer can show that the reason for it was one of the following:

(*a*) related to the employee's capability or qualification for the job;

(*b*) related to the employee's conduct (but *see* below);

(*c*) redundancy (*see* **5**);

(*d*) pursuant to a statutory duty or restriction on either employer or employee.

The Employment Act 1980 makes the onus of proof of "fairness" of a dismissal neutral as between employer and employee. (Under previous legislation the onus was on the employer to show that he acted "fairly".)

The following dismissals will be held as "unfair":

(*a*) When, on grounds of redundancy, an employee is selected for dismissal because of trade union membership or activities, or the employer ignored the agreed procedure for selection of employees for redundancy.

(*b*) If the employee was, or proposed to become a member of an independent trade union (a union which is not under employer domination or control), or took part in union activities, unless, in the absence of an arrangement with the employer, the activities were within working hours.

(*c*) If the employee refused to belong to a non-independent trade union.

The foregoing (*a*) and (*b*) are called "inadmissible reasons". Other inadmissible reasons include the case of an employee who, on grounds of conscience or other deeply held personal conviction, objects to membership of a "closed-shop" union agreement.

Dismissals on grounds of pregnancy, sex or race discrimination (note the Sex Discrimination Act 1975 and the Race Relations Act 1976) are also "unfair".

The Employment Act 1982 introduced important new rights for employees and employers. The Act gives employees the following rights.

(*a*) A right not to be unfairly dismissed in a closed shop which has not been approved in a ballot in the preceding 5 years.

(*b*) Not to be unfairly dismissed in a closed shop if they have been unreasonably excluded or expelled from a trade union.

(*c*) Not to be unfairly dismissed in a closed shop if there is a conflict between their membership of a trade union and their professional code of ethics.

(*d*) Not to be selected for redundancy on grounds of non-membership of a union.

(*e*) Section 4 of the Act introduces a maximum basic award of £2,000 for anyone who is unfairly dismissed either because of trade union membership or activities or because of non-membership of a union.

(*f*) Section 5 of the Act creates a new "special award" of compensation which is payable when a dismissed employee asks an industrial tribunal to order his reinstatement or re-engagement, but no reinstatement or re-engagement results. In the absence of an order by the tribunal, the amount of the award will be 104 weeks' pay subject to a minimum of £10,000 and a maximum of £20,000. If the employer refuses to implement an order by the tribunal, the amount of the "special award" will be 156 weeks' pay subject to a minimum of £15,000. The "special award" in both cases is additional to any basic or compensatory award. Any award may be reduced on account of matters such as the employee's conduct before dismissal.

(*g*) Sections 7 and 11 enable an employee who claims that he was unfairly dismissed or had other action taken against him for not being a member of a trade union to request a tribunal to "join" as a party to tribunal proceedings a trade union or other person that, he claims, put pressure on his employer to dismiss or take action against him by calling or threatening industrial action because he was not a union member. Where a trade union is "joined" in the proceedings and the tribunal finds that it did exert such pressure on the employer, the tribunal can award compensation wholly or partly against the union rather than against the employer.

(*h*) Section 9 amends the law relating to dismissal in connection with industrial action. It provides that an employee who is dismissed while participating in a strike or other industrial action cannot claim unfair dismissal if the following conditions have been met:

(*i*) his or her employer has dismissed all who were taking part in the action at the same establishment as the complainant at the date of his dismissal; and

(*ii*) his or her employer has not offered re-engagement to any of them within three months of their date of dismissal without making him/her a similar offer.

4. ACAS. A major purpose of the Employment Protection Act 1975 (now consolidated under the Employment Protection (Consolidation) Act 1978) is to encourage the extension of collective bargaining. The Advisory, Conciliation and Arbitration Service

(ACAS) was set up in 1975 on a statutory basis to offer industrial relations advice, to provide a conciliation service and to arrange for reference to arbitration by the Central Arbitration Committee (CAC).

5. Redundancy. Employers are required to consult appropriate trade unions whenever they propose to make even a single employee redundant. They must also notify the Secretary of State if they plan to make ten or more employees redundant at one establishment within a specified period. This obligation applies even when the person, or persons to be made redundant are volunteers.

An employer must make a lump-sum compensation to an employee, who is dismissed because of redundancy. The amount of the payment is related to age, pay and length of service. The Redundancy Fund is financed by an allocation from the earnings-related secondary Class I contributions paid by employers under the Social Security Act 1975. When the employee leaves, the employer pays the required compensation in full, but he is entitled to claim a rebate of part of it from the Fund.

6. Labour turnover. A useful formula to assess the relative stability of staff at different periods within the same organisation, or for comparison with other companies, notably those within the same group, is the *ratio* of staff separations compared with the *average* number of *full-time* staff, usually expressed over a set period (usually one year). The basic formula (similar to that employed to measure the rate of turnover of stock) is:

$$LTO = (100 \times R)/W$$

where R = replacements of staff, or new employees who replace staff leaving, and W = the average work force.

A refinement of this formula considers those employees who leave for unavoidable reasons, retirement, marriage, etc.

$$LTO = 100(R - U)/W$$

where U = the unavoidable separations.

7. Limitations of the formula. LTO applied to an annual set of labour statistics is of limited value in itself. It will be important to know also the seasonal pattern of staff separations, the sex, age and type of employees involved and the reasons for their departure.

8. The significance of labour turnover. A high rate of labour turnover is a matter of the greatest concern to the personnel officer because:

(*a*) it adds to the cost of recruitment (advertising, interviewing, taking up references, etc.);

(*b*) additional cost, in time and money, of training;

(*c*) loss of efficiency while new staff are being trained, additional overtime may have to be worked;

(*d*) it depresses the morale of the remaining employees;

(*e*) it impairs the prestige of the company;

(*f*) if the separations include dismissals there may be complications under the Employment Protection (Consolidation) Act 1978.

The rate of turnover is a major function of the national rate of unemployment, with which there is an inverse correlation.

9. Reasons for a high rate of labour turnover.

(*a*) Inadequate pay structure.

(*b*) Lack of proper training and poor promotion prospects, e.g. many dead-end jobs.

(*c*) Dull, monotonous work.

(*d*) Poor working conditions.

(*e*) Bad staff selection, leading to square pegs in round holes.

(*f*) Inequitable distribution of work.

(*g*) Harsh, unsympathetic supervision.

A combination of the above is readily conducive to bad morale among the staff. Labour turnover may remain low, however, in spite of some of the above disadvantages. Relative security in times of high unemployment, nearness to home and friends often persuade an employee to accept the evils that he knows, while a generous pension scheme is a powerful retaining force.

10. Staff morale. This is the collective attitude of employees towards their work, their employers, the management and to their working conditions.

"People like to take an interest in their work. They like to know to what they are contributing. They like to be able to appreciate the work of their hands. They like to be in a position to know when their work is good." (Lord Lindsay)

Excessive zeal on the part of an administration striving for greater efficiency may be conducive to greater concern for the performance of the work than for the well-being and happiness (work satisfaction) of the workers.

Low morale is apparent when the following occur.

(*a*) The rate of labour turnover is significantly higher than previously, or in comparable organisations.

(*b*) There is an increase in disciplinary actions.

(*c*) Poor quality work.

(*d*) Bad timekeeping.

(*e*) Lack of co-operation.

(*f*) Frequent periods of absence for one or two days because of "sickness".

(*g*) Poor human relations.

11. Finding reasons for low morale. Since low morale directly affects office efficiency it is imperative to find reasons for it, by doing one or more of the following.

(*a*) Interviewing all employees leaving. Many will give the wrong answer, or a superficial one, and therefore it is necessary for the interviewer to be tactful and impartial, especially when personal animosity is the reason for departure.

(*b*) Talking informally to employees on the job.

(*c*) Setting up a grievance committee.

(*d*) Using an attitude survey, or questionnaires, in which employees answer questions (anonymously) about their jobs, their employer and the management.

When dealing with people with "a chip on their shoulders", a kind and understanding attitude is necessary—it will help morale greatly if it is known that the personnel officer has the habit of saying, "don't sit down opposite me across the table—come and sit beside me".

12. Ways of improving morale.

(*a*) Offer at least the market rates of pay and conditions of work.

(*b*) Provide merit rating and realistic methods of promotion.

(*c*) Offer financial incentives (e.g. annual bonus).

(*d*) Provide good welfare facilities.

(*e*) Provide subsidised meals at the company canteen, or operate a luncheon vouchers scheme.

(*f*) Organise suggestion schemes.

(*g*) Systematic training schemes, with generous day-release facilities to local colleges.

(*h*) Joint consultation.

(*i*) Profit-sharing and co-partnership.

13. House Journals (or staff magazines).

(*a*) A house journal should be published at regular intervals.

(*b*) It should inform employees of current company policy.

(*c*) It should encourage a better understanding of management problems.

(*d*) It should counter rumours.

(*e*) It should promote better team spirit and goodwill towards the company.

14. Usual content of house journals and staff magazines.

(*a*) Company developments and changes in policy (new factory, shops, etc., with new opportunities for staff).

(*b*) Social news of marriages, deaths and retirement of staff.

(*c*) Sports and social club reports.

(*d*) News of examination successes at the local college affecting employees: details of current and prospective courses.

(*e*) General magazine content—photographs, competitions, etc.

15. Suggestion schemes. Such schemes are run with the object of:

(*a*) increasing the interest of employees in their work;

(*b*) increasing the efficiency of methods used; and

(*c*) giving some reward to the worker who makes good suggestions for work improvement.

Such a scheme takes the form of fixing suggestion boxes to walls in various parts of the business premises, in which are "posted" printed suggestion forms on which workers make their suggestions.

Areas of suggestions usually include improvements to existing methods, new ideas about the new designs for the products manufactured, savings in effort or material, prevention of waste, improvements in safety devices and improvements in materials handling.

16. Setting up a suggestion scheme.

(*a*) Hold a meeting of workers to explain the objects of the scheme.

(*b*) Get forms printed and suggestion boxes fixed.

(*c*) Appoint a committee to assess suggestions (usually something like the following: personnel manager, company secretary and foreman or supervisor of shop or office concerned).

(*d*) Decide on the frequency of meetings.

(*e*) Decide on the amount of cash awards.

(*f*) Decide on methods of maintaining interest in the scheme.

17. Principal rules for success with suggestion schemes.

(*a*) The scheme must have adequate publicity and the confidence of employees as well as of the management.

(*b*) The rules must be simple and generally understood.

(*c*) Suggestions must be tested where possible and adopted if approved (otherwise cynicism about the scheme is engendered).

(*d*) All suggestions must be dealt with quickly.

(*e*) Employees must be constantly stimulated to make fresh suggestions.

18. Suggestion schemes in the office. Suggestion schemes are not usually such a success in the office as in the factory because:

(*a*) suggestions are not likely to be forthcoming unless there are good cash awards (usually based on savings made);

(*b*) since it is difficult to measure actual savings made in the office, it is difficult to assess a basis for cash awards;

(*c*) office supervisors do not always encourage suggestions from employees (criticisms are often resented).

NOTE: The real value of suggestion schemes should be assessed not merely on the tangible results, but in terms of stimulating employees to take a greater interest in their work.

PROGRESS TEST 10

1. What must an employer do within 13 weeks of an employee starting work? (**2**)

2. Give three examples each of (*a*) fair dismissal; (*b*) unfair dismissal. (**3**)

3. What is ACAS? (**4**)

4. What must an employer do when he proposes to make (*a*) one, (*b*) ten or more, persons redundant? Is his obligation different if the person or persons volunteer for redundancy? (**5**)

5. Examine the major additional responsibilities imposed upon personnel officers by the legislation described in (**1–5**).

6. An employee alleges unfair dismissal. Has the employer any onus of proof that he acted "fairly"? (**3**)

7. If you are informed that the rate of turnover of labour in a particular company was 15 per cent for 1976, what additional information would you require in order to make a reasoned assessment of employment in the company? (**7**)

8. What are the major effects of a high rate of labour turnover? (**8**)

9. Examine the basic reasons for low morale of the staff. (**10**)

10. Apart from knowledge of Acts of Parliament, office procedures, etc., what single quality would you rank highly in the list of qualities of a Personnel Officer? (**11**)

11. Discuss the part played by "house journals" in maintaining high staff morale. (**13**)

12. Describe how you would set up a suggestion scheme. (**16**)

CHAPTER XI

Office Procedures

1. An office procedure (or system) is the *sequence* of steps (or operations) in which they are performed, and is concerned with *what* is done, *how* it is, *when* it is done, *where* it is done and *who* does it.

2. Importance of office systems. Good systems:

(*a*) make for *smoother working* of the office i.e. better flow of work;

(*b*) give better *control* on what is done, and how it is done;

(*c*) give rise to *economies* in general costs and overhead expenses;

(*d*) make for *better co-ordination* between different departments;

(*e*) assist in the *training* of new staff;

(*f*) are related to office forms, the essential tools of clerical work.

3. Principles of office systems.

(*a*) They should be simple, so as to relieve supervision.

(*b*) The best use should be made of specialisation.

(*c*) Avoidance of unnecessary writing, movement or effort.

(*d*) Seek the best flow of work and avoidance of "bottlenecks".

(*e*) Avoid duplication of work, particularly with forms.

(*f*) There should be as few exceptions to the rule as possible.

(*g*) Avoid unnecessary checking.

(*h*) Systems should be flexible and adaptable to changed conditions.

(*i*) Proper allocation of duties (junior work to juniors, etc.).

(*j*) They should give continuous control on work performed.

(*k*) Make the best use of office machines.

(*l*) Use the best sequence of operations.

(*m*) Every operation performed must advance the work, with the purpose in mind.

(*n*) Paper-work should be kept to a minimum.

(*o*) Make best use of the "principle of exception" (in brief, this means the recording of negatives, or exceptions, rather than the bulk of the positives).

4. Office manual (or procedure manual). This consists of a booklet (usually loose-leaf) containing:

(*a*) an outline of the organisation (duties of each post, but with no names);

(*b*) the systems or methods of dealing with the work;

(*c*) the forms to be used, and how;

(*d*) the date of issue, and under whose authority the manual was published;

(*e*) instructions on how to use the manual.

5. Advantages and disadvantages of office manuals.

(*a*) *Advantages.*

(*i*) Writing the procedures down causes re-examination of systems.

(*ii*) They assist equitable distribution of work.

(*iii*) They relieve supervision.

(*iv*) They assist in training of new staff.

(*v*) They help in training holiday reliefs (no one is indispensable).

(*b*) *Disadvantages.*

(*i*) The procedures are no better than the way they are written down.

(*ii*) The work content of jobs is not always static.

(*iii*) Preparing a manual is a lengthy job, and it frequently becomes out of date.

(*iv*) They may dampen or stifle workers' initiative.

(*v*) Many offices function well without written procedure manuals.

NOTE: Office manuals probably have the greatest advantage in a large organisation where they help in standardising methods and in giving control over what is done.

6. Technique for establishing and improving an office system.

(*a*) Study and *analyse* in detail the work being done (using suitable charts).

(*b*) Determine which parts of the work are *essential*, bearing in mind the purpose of the office.

(*c*) *Eliminate* unnecessary operations (are they used? what for? how often? and who by?).

(*d*) Consider all *alternative methods* for remaining operations.

(*e*) Select the *best method* for each operation, having regard to control, cost and staffing.

(*f*) Determine fair *work standards* for each operation for purposes of control and staffing.

(*g*) Calculate the *personnel* required and seek the right sequence of operations to give the smoothest flow of work.

(*h*) Design the *office lay-out*, having regard to flow of work.

(*i*) *Train personnel* and install new procedure.

7. Work charts. The purpose of a chart is to portray a system, or flow of work in a simple way. Study of the chart reveals any faults in the system, notably duplication and overlapping of work, backtracking of documents, "bottlenecks", etc. A major technique of comparatively recent origin is critical path analysis and network analysis which have been successfully applied to the installation of a better accounting system or the marketing of a new product, although it is equally applicable in studying any system requiring a number of contributory operations, each of which requires a specified time. The purpose of the analysis is to identify the chain of operations which will achieve the desired result in minimum time, having regard to all concurrent and successive jobs.

The charts of major importance in general use in planning and controlling office procedures are:

(*a*) *Network analysis* (*critical path*) *charts*.

(*b*) *Procedure flow charts* show how office forms and their different copies move from one department to another. They illustrate, e.g. flow of export documents, or share certificates, instruments of transfer, etc., through the respective systems.

(*c*) *Work distribution charts* show how different kinds of work are allocated to employees.

(*d*) *Production study charts* show the relative employment of machines and operators.

(*e*) *Movement diagrams* show how documents move from one desk to another on the floor plan of the office. These diagrams are especially useful in planning, or altering, the office lay-out.

(*f*) *Operation charts* show the distance moved and the timings of left and right hands in studying an individual's detailed work.

NOTE: Specimens of these charts are shown in *Office Management* by J. C. Denyer, revised by Josephine Shaw (Macdonald & Evans, 5th edition, 1980).

8. Word-processing and microprocessors. The introduction of word-processing (*see* XV) and microprocessors (*see* XXV) has revolutionised office procedures in large offices throughout the world. Routine clerical operations are replaced by automated processes capable of delivering perfect copies of letters, invoices, cash-flow statements, etc., in a fraction of the time previously taken by copy-typists and clerks.

Many existing office systems therefore will have to be radically changed, if not abandoned. In preparation for the introduction of the new devices the following basic steps are essential.

(*a*) Review all existing procedures: assess their efficiency and operating costs.

(*b*) Decide on changes and/or abandonment of procedures which will be necessary if word-processing and microprocessors are contemplated.

(*c*) Consider the compensation payable to any staff likely to be made redundant by impending changes. The compensation may well be considerable, especially if several long-serving members of staff are involved. This is a cost-factor to be borne in mind when making the final decision to change to new procedures.

The Organisation and Methods officer (*see* XIII) will be directly involved in the review of the existing procedures: the suppliers of the new installations will be willing to offer advice and help.

PROGRESS TEST 11

1. What is the importance of a good office system? (**2**)

2. What are the major disadvantages of an office manual? (**5**)

3. What are the major techniques for improving an office system? (**6**)

4. What is the purpose of critical path analysis? (**7**)

5. (*a*) For ISCA students. Draft a procedure flow chart to show the movement of the relevant forms during the process of certification and registration of transfer of shares. (*b*) For costing students. Draft a procedure flow chart to show the movement of relevant documents to produce a job costing statement. (**7**)

6. What frequent errors in office systems does a properly drawn work chart reveal? (**7**)

7. What is the most likely effect on a large office of the introduction of word-processing and micro-technology? (**8**)

CHAPTER XII

Work Control

1. Control. This is a major element of administration. It is a continuous process whereby the administrator is kept informed of what is going on, in order that he may be able to compare current activity with planned activity. Budgetary control is a concrete example of how current costs are compared with standard costs and the variances noted.

Cybernetics is the science of systems of communication and control. The word is derived from the Greek word for steersman —one skilled in keeping a ship on course, and capable of correcting any deviation from course.

Word-processing and microprocessors (*see* XV and XXV) progressively render obsolete many of the methods described here. The need for quantity control is much reduced in view of the prodigious speed of performance, e.g. the average typist produces about 10 to 13 words per minute: word-processing devices type an error-free 350 words per minute.

The visual display unit facilitates immediate detection of errors of every kind in the original draft, so that quality control of work becomes academic in the large office. The need for work control will, however, persist in the non-automated office.

2. Exercise of control. Control is exercised over:

 (*a*) the *quantity* of work performed;
 (*b*) the *quality* of work performed;
 (*c*) the time element, or *scheduling*.

3. Quantity control. This is not of general application to the output of an office. Scientific control of output is feasible only where work is routine and repetitive, and where standard times for performance of units of output have been defined. There is a wide range of office jobs, however, to which quantity control can be, and ought to be, applied. These include:

 (*a*) typing of routine documents;
 (*b*) envelope addressing;
 (*c*) embossing addressing-machine plates;

(d) ledger posting;

(e) punching cards, etc.

While it may not be feasible to apply quantity control to the work of an individual, it may be entirely practicable and, indeed, necessary, to apply it to the work of the department.

NOTE: Note the underlying principle of the stability of large numbers.

4. Examples of simple measurement of office work.

(a) By comparing first and last numbers of pre-numbered documents, e.g. orders, invoices, etc. Allow for the possibility of spoiled documents, which the clerk has surreptitiously destroyed.

(b) By issuing work in standard batches, e.g. dictating machine recordings.

(c) By using plastic grids ruled in square inches (Leffingwell-Ream) to measure typed material on business letters. Differing styles of type face such as pica (10 characters per 25 mm) and elite (12 characters per 25 mm) must be considered.

(d) By weighing documents, and comparing with standard weight equated to quantity, e.g. for filing of records.

Effective quantity control requires routine reports at regular intervals: e.g.

Number of invoices in hand at beginning of day		a
Plus Number received during day		b
		a + b
Less Number passed	c	
Less Number scrapped	d	c + d
Number in hand at end of day		(a + b) − (c + d)

5. Dealing with bottlenecks.
A bottleneck occurs in an office when the work piles up at a certain point causing delays in the smooth flow of documents, e.g. when a clerk is flooded with an unusual amount of work, or has encountered a snag not easily resolved. Methods of avoiding bottlenecks include:

(a) devise a smooth flow of work when planning the system;

(b) maintain effective quantity control;

(c) introduce machines to quicken the flow of work, but have emergency plans for breakdown of a machine;

(d) avoid too much specialisation, so that a vacancy caused by sudden illness, for example, can be filled by a competent "all-rounder";

(e) use cycle-billing for sales invoicing (the sending out of monthly statements according to a cycle throughout the month, instead of waiting until the end of the month);

(f) stagger dividend and interest payments throughout the year: to pay ordinary and preference interim dividends and half-yearly debenture interest all on the same day may unnecessarily congest the office.

6. Quality control. Some clerical errors of all types are unavoidable: every attempt must none the less be made to keep them to a minimum and to make very sure that they do not pass undetected.

It is necessary to define for each job, to which quality control is to be applied, the acceptable percentage of errors, e.g. a supervisor checking the typescript of an average typist is prepared to accept a standard of quality of not more than 3 errors per 1000 words. Errors occurring in routine, repetitive work are usually distributed according to the Poisson distribution, standard tables of which are available (J. Murdoch and J. A. Barnes, *Statistical Tables*, 2nd edition, Macmillan). In the present case, the probability that the typist, in typing 1000 words, will exceed 3 errors is 0.3528. The probability that she will exceed 5 errors is only 0.0839. Suppose the supervisor, while checking a sample of current typescript finds more than 5 errors then an 8 per cent chance has materialised. The vital step now is to decide (and this is largely arbitrary) whether this result is significant, that is attributable to something other than the fluctuations of random sampling, e.g. lack of concentration because of illness on the part of the typist.

Quality control is a highly specialised branch of statistics and should not be undertaken without guidance from a qualified statistician.

7. Causes of error in clerical work. The quality of clerical work is often measured by the incidence of errors, attributable to:

(a) *Fault of the worker:*
   (i) being too hasty;
   (ii) lack of method in working;
   (iii) carelessness;
   (iv) lack of theoretical knowledge;
   (v) bad figures and bad handwriting;
   (vi) laziness;
   (vii) fatigue;

(*viii*) poor health;

(*ix*) disaffection (showing perhaps the first signs of lowering of staff morale).

  (*b*) *Fault of the management:*

    (*i*) bad staff selection;

    (*ii*) indifferent induction and training policy;

    (*iii*) lack of communication of management policy;

    (*iv*) low staff morale;

    (*v*) understaffing;

    (*vi*) inadequate checking.

8. Work checking. The relative importance of work to be checked determines whether hundred per cent checking or checking by sample is to be applied.

Hundred per cent checking may be burdensome where a great volume of work is involved. There is no assurance that checking everything will necessarily reveal errors, for there is the risk that the checker will become bored and fail to detect a mistake.

There is a strong case for random sampling part of the bulk and deducing from the result of the sample the quality of the bulk.

NOTE: Random sampling, using, for example, Tippett's table of random numbers (L. H. C. Tippett, *Random Sampling*, Cambridge University Press, 1927), means that every item in the bulk has an equal chance of being included in the sample.

Random sampling is subject to error, i.e. the sample may not be truly representative of the bulk, and, accordingly two risks may be defined:

  (*a*) *Checker's risk*—that he may accept a bad batch of work on the faith of the good sample; and

  (*b*) *Clerk's risk*—that his good batch of work will be rejected by the checker on the faith of a bad sample.

Statistical quality control is now regularly employed in many large offices. Note that unless sampling is truly random, statistical quality control is ineffective.

9. Time scheduling. This third control consists of budgeting the quantities of work for performance within certain times and then comparing the actual performance with the budgeted quantities. Useful graphical effect is given to this form of control by the Gantt chart, an example of which is shown in Fig. 3.

In Fig. 3, at the end of week 5, the supervisor notes with

Week No.	Budget units of Output	Actual units of output	Weekly %	Cumulative %	
1	400	350	87½	87½	
2	500	600	120	100	+10
3	500	400	80	90	
4	450	600	133½	100	+20
5	500	550	110	100	+33⅓
6	450	—			

Week No.	1	2	3	4	5	6
Budget	400	500	500	450	500	450
Actual	350	600	400	600	550	
Weekly %						
Cumulative %						

FIG. 3   *An example of a Gantt chart.*

satisfaction that production is not only level with the budget but 150 units of week 6 have been completed as well, i.e. $33\frac{1}{3}$ per cent of that week's budget of 450 units. This was achieved in spite of shortfalls in weeks 1 and 3, when, presumably, the exception principle of management was invoked to apply emergency measures to correct the disparity.

PROGRESS TEST 12

1. Give four examples of simple measuring methods of office output. **(2)**

2. What is the potential danger of too much specialisation in an office? **(5)**

3. What is: (*a*) an acceptable percentage of errors, (*b*) a significant percentage of errors? **(6)**

4. State, preferably from your own experience, four major causes of error in clerical work. **(7)**

5. What are the objections to hundred per cent checking of clerical work? **(8)**

6. What is recorded on a Gantt chart, and for what purpose? **(9)**

CHAPTER XIII

Work Simplification (O & M)

1. Work simplification (or O & M—Organisation and Methods). This is the scientific checking of the efficiency of office work.

Its scope includes everything that contributes to efficiency (*see* **I, 5**), but in particular it deals with office organisation, office systems, methods, machines and equipment, office forms and work measurement.

2. Objectives.

(*a*) To reduce the cost of office work to the minimum.

(*b*) To establish the most efficient procedures for paperwork.

(*c*) To release staff, office space and finance and use them for other perhaps more important operations.

(*d*) To provide management with the right control information at the right time.

(*e*) To ensure that office administration achieves its purposes.

NOTE: Efficiency can be interpreted in different ways.

(1) The same volume of work with less staff and at less expense.

(2) A greater volume of work with a less than proportionate increase of effort.

(3) Achievement of the purposes of the office with greater outlay in the interests of improving human relationships.

3. Setting up O & M. This is usually done by a separate officer or department (called the Work Study Officer or the O & M Department). The terms *O & M, work study* and *work simplification* are synonymous. Such officer or department should be responsible to general management and not to any specific department or of course their allegiance will be biased. Many companies employ outside O & M consultants for a major assessment and to obtain recommendations for a revision of the existing system.

Sometimes the O & M chief reports to regular meetings of a committee composed of himself, the company secretary and, say, the chief accountant. He then reports his progress and submits his plans for confirmation by such committee.

A most important aspect is the explanation of the function and authority of the department to the rest of the staff, in order to allay fear and suspicion.

This can be helped by:

(*a*) giving two or three day appreciation courses to all supervisors and above throughout the company; and

(*b*) by the giving of guarantees to the staff that:

(*i*) all redundant employees will be absorbed through wastage in other departments;

(*ii*) the function of O & M is purely advisory and no changes can be implemented without the approval of the manager of the department concerned;

(*iii*) there will be no recrimination against employees.

4. Why have O & M? Independent O & M officers or departments are necessary because:

(*a*) they have the time in which to make the inquiries (heads of departments rarely do);

(*b*) they are independent and need not think of their own positions;

(*c*) they can view the work objectively;

(*d*) they bring to the study their specialised experience in other departments or businesses.

5. O & M technique. An O & M assignment may be for a single procedure in an office (or for the whole office), and the assignment usually falls into the following steps:

(*a*) *Determining the objects* of the assignment and defining them in writing.

(*b*) *Planning the assignment*, which will depend on how large the assignment is.

(*c*) *Collecting the facts*, which may be done by personal observation, by interviews with staff or by issuing questionnaires.

(*d*) *Analysing the facts*, which is preparatory to work improvement. Here, questions are asked as to what is done, why it is done, when and where it is done, who does it, and how it is done.

(*e*) After improvements have been envisaged, the *proposals are then submitted* for subsequent action. Usually, the comments of managers concerned are attached when submitted to top management.

6. Advantages of O & M.

(a) Improves general efficiency of the office as a whole (note the meaning of efficiency in **2** above).

(b) Checks wasteful expenditure, the use of unnecessary clerical labour and unnecessary records.

(c) Makes for savings in overhead expenses, stationery and labour costs.

(d) Assists management in its assessment of office work and systems.

(e) Keeps staff "efficiency-minded".

7. Disadvantages and difficulties.

(a) Tends to be a rather dehumanised inquiry.

(b) It is not easy to assess the efficiency of an office on the findings of a few short visits only, although it is possible that "onlookers see more of the game than the players".

(c) What seems reasonable in theory is often unworkable in practice.

(d) It instils a feeling of insecurity in staff who are subject to O & M inquiries and lowers morale.

(e) Tendency of O & M experts to view themselves as a part of management, instead of merely advisory to them.

8. Success of O & M. Success depends greatly on the following conditions:

(a) It should be applied sensibly and resourcefully by men of the right calibre, well aware of the need to maintain the right balance between the worker and the work.

(b) Its purpose should be fully understood and accepted by the people whose jobs are examined.

(c) The project should be actively supported by top management.

9. O & M and paperwork. Office forms are closely related to office systems. Every office form in use means clerical staff to fill it in, to handle it and file it. Therefore the fewer the forms the better.

Reduction of paperwork is often a main method of effecting economies, which depend on:

(a) degree of central control by management;

(b) amount of duplication of records;

(c) investigation of purpose of forms;

(*d*) proper forms control (often exercised by O & M);

(*e*) degree of formality in office work required by management.

10. The automated office. The rapid expansion of word-processing and micro-technology (*see* XV and XXV) has had a far-reaching effect on the scope and nature of Organisation and Method. Traditional work-patterns of clerical workers, from management levels down to clerks and typists are being analysed, and in many offices fundamentally changed or abandoned. The O & M department will necessarily be directly involved in any proposed introduction of modern systems (*see* XI).

PROGRESS TEST 13

1. Why, necessarily, is there more than one definition of office efficiency? **(2)**

2. What are the major objectives of O & M? **(2)**

3. Argue the case for the employment of outside O & M consultants. **(3, 7)**

4. Do you agree, from your own experience, that outsiders are likely to note quickly the nature and degree of inefficiency in an office? **(7)**

5. What is needed to ensure the success of an O & M investigation? **(8)**

6. Why does an O & M investigation regard forms as important? **(9)**

PART TWO

OFFICE EQUIPMENT

CHAPTER XIV

Office Machines

1. Introduction. The provision and use of office machinery combines labour and capital in the pursuit of greater efficiency, and what is true of machine tools in the factory is equally true of the many types of machines in the office, namely, that a machine has to earn its keep.

No machine is worth purchasing unless it can be shown by careful analysis by the O & M team that efficiency is thereby improved.

The rapid development of word-processing (*see* XV) and microtechnology (*see* XXV) has already displaced many of the office machines described in the following chapters. In particular, manual typewriters are being phased out of mass production and their use will survive only in small offices.

To comply with examination syllabuses, however, existing machinery will be described, but the student must clearly understand that much of it will be obsolete shortly.

2. Advantages of office machines.

(*a*) They normally save labour by releasing staff for other work. It is, however, sometimes found that additional staff are required, e.g. when a computer is installed, but since a great deal of additional information, including valuable management statistics is provided much more quickly than was previously possible, a like-with-like comparison is not possible.

(*b*) They save time. This is an important advantage when a deadline has to be beaten, e.g. end of month balancing, payment of wages, etc.

(*c*) They promote accuracy. Accounting machines in particular have a running check on the accuracy of their output.

(*d*) They relieve the drudgery of conventional hand-written methods.

(*e*) They enhance the appearance of output, especially letters typed on variable type, right-hand justification machines. The company's image is thereby maintained.

(*f*) Some devices, e.g. cheque-writing machines, *avoid fraud*.

(*g*) They lessen the fatigue of the staff and thereby improve the quality of output (e.g. electric typewriters).

3. Disadvantages of office machines.

(*a*) Machines cannot do work requiring great intelligence (electronic computers are colloquially called "Tom"—"thoroughly obedient moron"). No machine, however sophisticated, can produce a better output than the input deserves.

(*b*) Many machines, notably electronic machines, rapidly become obsolescent.

(*c*) Expense of:

   (*i*) special stationery and printing.

   (*ii*) training machine operators, or paying high salaries to attract trained personnel.

(*d*) Impact on the existing system. Some installations revolutionise a system and staff may be antagonised.

(*e*) Many machines are less mobile between departments than clerks.

(*f*) The machine enforces its own rigid pattern upon the system which is therefore less flexible than previously.

(*g*) Some machines are noisy, take up room, need regular attention.

(*h*) High capital outlay.

(*i*) Maintenance is usually costly; breakdowns may be disastrous.

4. Installation. The decision to buy and install a machine is taken only if the following questions can be answered affirmatively:

(*a*) Is the present method inefficient?

(*b*) Will the machine improve the output?

(*c*) Will increased efficiency (including more management statistics) justify the cost of the machine?

(*d*) Will trained staff be available: is space available?

(*e*) Have all relevant questions been asked:

   (*i*) about the life of the machine;

   (*ii*) about the possibility of leasing, instead of buying it;

   (*iii*) will a better machine shortly be on the market?

The final decision may be assisted by a careful study of the break-even chart given in Fig. 4. Assuming other things being

Choice of machine (e.g. for wage calculation)

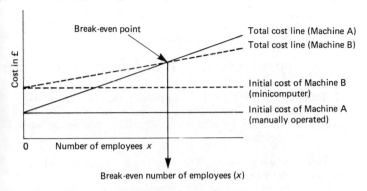

FIG. 4 *Break-even chart.*

equal, the company is advised to purchase machine B (the mini-computer) when expansion takes the pay-roll above *x* employees.

PROGRESS TEST 14

1. Discuss the contention that office machinery puts clerks out of work. (**2**)

2. To what extent does machinery affect the company's public relationships? (**2**)

3. What effect is a large machine installation likely to have on human relations in the office? (**2, 3**)

4. State the major disadvantages of office machinery. (**3**)

5. Hasty decisions are often taken about buying office machinery. How would you avoid making such decisions? (**4**)

6. Draft a "decision chart" to enable a decision to be made between Machine X and Machine Y, given the following facts:

	Machine X	*Machine Y*
	£	£
Initial cost	1000	1500
Annual cost of entry per employee	2	1.6
Life of machine	4 years	3 years

The company currently employs 1,200 persons. (**4**).

CHAPTER XV

Typewriters and Word-processing

1. Introduction. The typewriter is probably the most widely used office machine. Its use displaces the much slower handwritten communication and the wide choice of models available give work of better appearance.

2. Buying a new typewriter. The following basic questions should be asked, and factors should be considered.

(*a*) Is an extra typewriter necessary, or can the existing typists be deployed (through flexitime, etc.) to use the present machines?

NOTE: Some aspect of "double-shift" use of capital equipment is possible with a properly organised flexitime system.

(*b*) Is space available?

(*c*) What are the special requirements of the work for which the new machine is needed?

    (*i*) Long carriage for legal documents?

    (*ii*) Heavy pressure for many copies?

    (*iii*) Variable type-face?

    (*iv*) Half-spacing?

(*d*) Capital cost—will the budget accommodate the outlay?

(*e*) Maintenance, guarantee and period of delivery?

(*f*) Wishes of the long-service typist?

(*g*) Is the noise likely to disturb other workers?

(*h*) Pleasing design and appearance? Easy to clean?

3. Electric typewriters. These are typewriters on which the throw of the type-bars is actuated by the electric motor.

(*a*) Some machines have space bar, carriage return, tabulator, etc., also electrically operated.

(*b*) Only light depression of the keys is necessary to operate an electric typewriter.

(*c*) Margin justification (straight right-hand margin) and differential space justification are obtainable on some machines. The latter feature varies the spacing of letters according to their width, giving the appearance of the printed page.

(*d*) *Applications.* Can be used wherever a standard typewriter is used, but particularly suitable for stencils, invoicing and preparation of material for printing.

(*e*) *Advantages.*

(*i*) Perfectly even impression with printed appearance.

(*ii*) Up to 20 carbon copies obtainable.

(*iii*) Good for typing stencils (even impression).

(*iv*) Lessens fatigue of typists and thus improves quality of work.

(*f*) *Disadvantages.*

(*i*) Typists take some time in getting used to the light touch.

(*ii*) Generally more expensive than standard typewriters.

4. Variable-type machines. These are typewriters on which different sizes and styles of type are available, all on the same machine.

(*a*) Different type segments, each bearing all the characters in a particular typeface, are interchangeable in seconds.

(*b*) Such machines are electrically operated and usually give differential space justification and margin justification.

(*c*) *Applications.* Mainly as composing machines for the preparation of masters for offset-litho machines, where it is invaluable to be able to type different sizes and styles of type.

(*d*) They can also be used for special report work, minutes, etc.

(*e*) Since they cost four to five times as much as ordinary typewriters, their cost would not be justified unless used for such special purposes.

5. Automatic typewriters. These are typewriters which, when plain paper is fed into the machine, automatically type a standard letter, paragraph, etc., at about 350 words per minute.

The distinctive feature of the Selectric typewriter introduced in the early 1960s is the spinning "golfball" element containing type. Unlike the standard typewriter, of which the carriage moves when a key is depressed, the Selectric has no moving carriage. The "golf-ball" moves across the face of the paper, spinning around to present the correct character. The elimination of the heavy moving carriage (c/f for legal documents) permits higher typing speeds. On a Selectric, a good typist's speed can be increased by 50 per cent or more.

Variations of the "golf-ball" are the "daisy wheel" and the "thimble" elements. These are widely used in word-processing. The element can be quickly changed to provide a different typeface with, for example, mathematical symbols or Cyrillic script.

(*a*) They are usually operated by a prepared reel of punched paper tape (punched on a special machine), which can then be stored and used again for automatic re-typing of the standard letter when required (some now use magnetic tape).

(*b*) A special kind of automatic typewriter gives a selection from a hundred or more push buttons. Each button when depressed reproduces a standard paragraph, the machine having a total capacity of 500 typewritten lines.

(*c*) *Applications.* For any standard letter, etc., it is wished to reproduce to meet recurring similar situations (addressees' names and addresses can be typed in individually), and where it is wished for this letter, etc., to have a typed appearance.

(*d*) *Particular examples.*

(*i*) Communications with shareholders of a large company.

(*ii*) Direct mail selling.

(*iii*) Letters of quotation.

(*iv*) Export sales letters.

(*v*) Invitations to tender.

(*vi*) Credit letters in a series.

6. Typing pool. This is where all (or most) of the typists in an organisation work in one room together instead of in separate offices, and where the work is shared among them.

(*a*) *Advantages.*

(*i*) Makes the most economical use of typists.

(*ii*) More even distribution of work.

(*iii*) Minimises difficulties due to absence to typists (sickness and holidays).

(*iv*) Better training can be provided for juniors.

(*v*) Junior duties e.g. answering the telephone, can be delegated to juniors.

(*vi*) Working conditions appropriate to typists can be provided.

(*vii*) The noise of typing is confined to one room.

(*viii*) Improved supervision.

(*ix*) Typists have opportunity for wider experience.

(*b*) *Disadvantages.*

(*i*) Lack of personal contact of typists with executives.

(*ii*) Not suitable where private secretaries are employed.

(*iii*) It may encourage gossiping.

(*iv*) It may not suffice where specialised work is involved.

(*v*) Lack of continuity of interest on the part of typists.

(*vi*) Delays caused by calling typists from the pool.

(*vii*) If not already in being, a messenger service will be required to take finished letters back to departments.

NOTE: It is possible to compromise by having a typing pool, but one where an individual service is offered.

7. Establishing a typing pool. Factors to consider when establishing a typing pool are:

(*a*) Are some typists in some departments overworked while others in other departments are under-employed?

(*b*) Is the noise of typing disturbing to others?

(*c*) Is there an organised training scheme for juniors?

(*d*) Whether the number of typists is increasing, and it is wished to restrict their numbers.

(*e*) Whether it is wished to improve supervision of typists.

(*f*) Whether typists are engaged in junior clerical work.
Practical factors include:

(*g*) Is there a large enough room to accommodate the number of typists required (and is the room centrally sited)?

(*h*) Has it been decided what policy to adopt regarding private secretaries?

(*i*) Is there an employee suitable for appointment as supervisor?

(*j*) Financial factors, such as: will the typists want an increase in pay to retain them? the cost of a supervisor; the cost of a messenger service, etc.

Following the introduction of word-processing the size of the typing-pool tends to be reduced and the function of the typist fundamentally altered.

8. Word-processing. This truly remarkable technique followed the invention of the automatic electric typewriter. It provides:

(*a*) The typing of an error-free letter, specification, invoice, etc. at 350+ words per minute. (An average typist, using conventional methods, will produce around 10 to 13 words a minute).

(*b*) The storage and instantaneous retrieval of information. It will store whatever is typed into it—complete documents by character, word, line, paragraph and page on magnetic card or tape cassette. The card stores up to four A4 pages—the cassette up to 25 letter-size documents. Corrections, amendments and additions (e.g. the updating of prices) are easily effected.

(*c*) It will produce a perfectly-printed annual report or bulk mailings each one of which is typed as an original with a different address automatically typed in. No operator need be in attendance.

(*d*) When the original is typed (using, of course, the "golfball" or the unique "daisy wheel" element) the line feed automatically activates near the margin when a word has been typed, so that the typist does not have to worry about line breaks.

(*e*) On the recall of information from store the device prints the first line left to right, the second right to left, and so on.

(*f*) Full-display screens present an instant picture of documents being typed, recalled, amended and corrected. Therefore no paper need be used when drafting, formatting is easier and typing speeds are increased, because the user always gets clear visual feedback and reassurance.

(*g*) The system is designed with simple, self-checking features built in to pinpoint problems and hasten repairs (replacement parts required are even displayed on the screen!!).

(*h*) The manufacturer of the system trains the company's operators with courses to accord with individual requirements.

(*i*) Most manufacturers offer outright purchase or rental of the system. Rental pricing schemes include service and parts.

PROGRESS TEST 15

1. For what kinds of work is it necessary to have:
(*a*) electric typewriters; (*b*) variable-type typewriters; (*c*) long-carriage typewriters? (**1, 3, 4**)

2. What kind of typewriter would you recommend for: (*a*) direct mail selling; (*b*) invitations to tender debentures for redemption; (*c*) notice of an extraordinary general meeting to shareholders of a public company? (**6**)

3. What are the major disadvantages of a typing pool? (**8**)

4. Discuss the contention that a typing pool provides typists with opportunities for wider experience. (**8**)

5. What considerations would guide you in the decision to set up a typing pool? (**9**)

6. Summarise the basic advantages of a word-processing system. (**8**)

7. A company sends out 1000 price lists every month to its customers. Describe how this may be done by word-processing. (**8**)

8. What part is played in word-processing by visual display units (screens)? (**8**)

9. To what extent does word-processing remove the need for elaborate work-control systems?

10. How is the work of the training officer simplified on the introduction of a word-processing system? **(8)**

11. In addition to time saved, what other economies may be achieved by word-processing?   **(8)** (*See also* **XI, 10**)

CHAPTER XVI

Dictating Machines

1. Definition. An electronic machine which records speech on one of various possible recording media, so that a typist can then play back the recording and transcribe it on her typewriter.

2. Different recording media.

(*a*) *Magnetic* (the most popular), on wire, plastic tape, plastic discs, paper sheet or plastic belts.

The great advantage of magnetic recording is that one can record on top of anything previously recorded, so that the same medium can be used over and over again, e.g. the "Thought Master" uses standard C-type tape cassettes, and accent throughout is on convenience for the busy top executive or high-volume dictator, and their equally busy secretaries.

(*b*) *Inscribed method*, on plastic discs or belts, where a track is cut in the plastic (as on a gramophone record) and the medium can only be used once. This could be claimed as an advantage because the recordings are then filed for reference purposes, often instead of carbon copies of the correspondence. This is obviously a more expensive method, but on the other hand it may be useful to have a permanent record of recordings made.

Recording time of the machines varies from 10 minutes to $8\frac{1}{2}$ hours, but the normal is about 10 to 20 minutes. The shorter recording time is more convenient because it enables quite a number of letters to be recorded, which can then be passed to a typist while another recording is being made.

3. Operational features. When describing a dictating machine, it would be necessary to include the usual operational features.

(*a*) Ability to record, play back and back-space (for re-hearing).

(*b*) Facility for locating any part of the dictated material (normally by use of index strip and scale indication on the machine).

(*c*) Dictation can be played back through ear-phones or, more usually, through stethophones.

(*d*) The typist usually controls the play-back by a foot control by which she can start, stop and back-space.

(*e*) Erasing facility, by which a recording can be cleaned off, e.g. if it is confidential information.

(*f*) An attachment to the telephone can be used which automatically records both sides of a telephone conversation.

(*g*) The machine can often be run off the mains, from dry batteries or from a car battery.

4. Uses of dictating machines.

(*a*) Dictation of routine correspondence.

(*b*) Recording of conferences.

(*c*) Recording of interviews or telephone conversations.

(*d*) Use in cars by sales representatives for recording sales reports.

(*e*) For speech and sales training.

(*f*) Convenient for business men when travelling abroad (to record business reports).

(*g*) For stocktaking purposes. Instead of it being a two-man job, one counting and the other recording, one man counts and records stock on his pocket dictating machine. Similarly, an estate agent can rapidly compile the inventory of furniture, etc., of a house.

(*h*) Market research, e.g. trial car drivers record their reactions when testing new cars.

5. Choosing a machine.
The main differences between machines on the market are as follows.

(*a*) Capital outlay and running costs (the inscribed method is more expensive to run than a magnetic machine).

(*b*) Fidelity of recording.

(*c*) Length of recording. Normally short recordings are suitable for correspondence and longer ones for records of meetings, etc.

(*d*) Weight (for portability).

(*e*) Simplicity of operation.

(*f*) Additional operational features, e.g. one machine has an automatic marking device on the index strip.

6. Making corrections.
There are two methods of making corrections:

(*a*) To over-record a correction on top of the mistake. This is possible only with the magnetic type; it takes time and is difficult to do.

(*b*) To include corrections at the end of the recording and mark the index strip where the corrections occur, as a warning to the typist.

7. Advantages and disadvantages of using dictating machines.

(*a*) *Advantages.*

(*i*) Economy in time of the dictater as well as of the typist. Usually the use of a dictating machine and audiotypists (instead of shorthand typists) means a saving of 50 per cent in typist staff.

(*ii*) Convenience to the dictator, who can dictate when he likes, where he likes and at any speed.

(*iii*) Various uses of the machines (*see* **4** above).

(*iv*) In typing pools it enables typing to be shared more easily among the typists, and overcomes the difficulties of reading other people's shorthand.

(*v*) The recordings offer a fairly simple method of measuring the work of typists.

(*vi*) It improves the supervision of typists as they have no occasion to be absent from the office to take letters down in shorthand.

(*b*) *Disadvantages.*

(*i*) Typists generally dislike dictating machines. They lose their speed at shorthand and are "tied" to the machine.

(*ii*) It requires training of dictators more than of typists.

(*iii*) Typists are not in close contact with executives so there is loss of personal contact.

(*iv*) It may make for lack of continuity of interest of typists in work performed.

(*v*) Difficulties of machine breakdown or power failure.

8. Central dictating system.
In a big business concern it would be uneconomic to provide every dictator with a recording machine, and a central dictating system entails the provision of a number of recording machines in the typing pool, connected by wire to a large number of offices so that recordings can be made by remote control.

Usually one recording machine is found sufficient for six to eight dictators.

9. Types of central dictating installation.
Two main types of installation are available:

(*a*) *Multi-bank.*

(*i*) The recording machines are in one big installation in the typing pool but separate from the typists.

(*ii*) The typists have separate play-back machines on their desks.

(*iii*) Dictators are automatically routed to a free machine for recording.

(*iv*) This system requires the supervisor to distribute the recordings to typists in proper sequence.

(*v*) It is probably the most economical method of installation where there is a large number of dictators.

(*b*) *Tandem installation.*

(*i*) Each typist has two machines on her desk, one for recording and one for play-back.

(*ii*) Usually this method has telephone connection as well, so that the dictator can give verbal typing instructions.

(*iii*) Dictators are automatically routed to a free machine.

(*iv*) It means the ratio of recording to transcribing machines is 1:1, and is perhaps only suitable for relatively small offices.

10. Methods of connection. In central dictating systems there are three methods of connection between the dictator and the recording machines:

(*a*) by hand-microphones hanging on the wall;

(*b*) by contact through the internal house telephone (PAX);

(*c*) by contact through the British Telecom telephone installation (PABX).

Provided permission is obtained from British Telecom, (*c*) is probably the most economical method of connection, but where the tandem system is preferred, then (*c*) or (*b*) would be used.

11. Advantages and disadvantages of central dictating system.

(*a*) *Advantages.*

(*i*) Convenience to the dictator: telephone, etc., right to hand.

(*ii*) Fewer machines are required than otherwise.

(*iii*) Recordings do not have to be sent to the typing pool: they are made in the typing pool.

(*iv*) All other advantages as in 7 above.

(*b*) *Disadvantages.*

(*i*) It may be expensive to install.

(*ii*) Dictation is restricted to rooms connected to the system. This may be inconvenient when rooms are changed.

(*iii*) Extra work is placed on the supervisor of the typing pool.

(*iv*) At busy times of the day "queueing" for the free machine may result, with consequent problems of priority. Queueing should be reduced, however, by a judicious use of flexible working hours.

(*v*) With some systems, the absence of index slips, of any
indication of the length of letters to typists and of corrections
may necessitate first playing through the whole recording.

(*vi*) A dictater who is interrupted may engage a machine
for longer than necessary, because it is inconvenient to make re-
connection.

(*vii*) After working hours the use of the system is limited to the
amount of recording medium left on the machines.

(*viii*) On some systems there is lack of indication that the
recording medium has come to an end.

12. Cassettes, word-processing and microprocessing. Cassettes play
an important part in word-processing (*see* XV) and microprocessing (*see* XXV). A recent example, among very many, is the
"Network" remote dictation system by means of which users are
able to communicate directly with the transcription supervisor to
clarify or issue new instructions on work that has been placed on
the machine.

"Network" is designed around a microprocessor. This provides
a high degree of personalised services not previously attainable.

In combination with the standard PABX, (*see* XXXI, **4**) touch-
tone and remote telephone systems Network will accept dictation
from anywhere in the country, which makes it ideal for use by
large companies which have external personnel as well as internal
dictation requirements.

The rapid development of word-processing and microprocessing
will render obsolete many of the dictating devices described in this
chapter, although their use is likely to persist for some years in non-
automated offices.

PROGRESS TEST 16

1. Discuss the various types of dictating machine and the
features which make one machine more suitable than others for
particular tasks. (**1**)

2. Explain the working of a dictating machine and how corrections are usually made. (**3, 6**)

3. Dictating machines are used for the recording of routine
correspondence: what other uses are there? (**4**)

4. What economies and other advantages would you expect to
derive from the introduction of dictating machines? (**7**)

5. Write a short report recommending the purchase of dictating
machines for your business. (**7, 8**)

6. Describe central dictating and outline the different methods available for its installation.   **(8–10)**

7. What do you consider are the advantages and disadvantages of a central dictating machine system?   **(11)**

CHAPTER XVII

Continuous Stationery

1. Definition. Continuous stationery is a device by which office forms are produced in a continuous strip; individual forms are usually divided from each other by perforations, and several copies of each form are produced simultaneously.

2. Methods of copying. When producing forms by continuous stationery, copies can be obtained in different ways.

(a) *One-time carbon.*

(i) This is interleaved by the manufacturers between the various copies of the forms.

(ii) This saves the insertion of carbon and has to be taken out only on completion of typing.

(b) *Carbon backing* (or spot carbon).

(i) This is where carbon is blocked on to the back of one paper.

(ii) When entries are made on the front, it automatically produces a carbon copy on the sheet below it.

(c) *Carbon pocket* (or jacket).

(i) This is a device whereby sheets of heavy carbon are interleaved between the forms.

(ii) When one form has been completed the carbon set, controlled by springs, is pulled back between the next set of forms to be typed.

(iii) When used up, the carbon set has then to be replaced.

(iv) This is a less expensive method than carbon backing.

(v) It also saves labour in insertion and extraction of carbons, but suffers from the carbon copies becoming progressively weaker.

(d) *"NCR"* ("No Carbon Required").

(i) This is paper, the underside of which is coated with a chemical, and the uppermost side of the paper underneath is similarly treated with a chemical.

(ii) When the top copy is typed on, it automatically creates a carbon copy on the sheet beneath by the interaction of these two chemicals.

(iii) This has the advantage of eliminating carbon completely.

(*iv*) Care must be taken in handling it (because it marks).

(*v*) It is relatively expensive.

3. Importance of continuous stationery.

(*a*) Where a large volume of work is required on standard business forms, it saves a great deal of labour costs (*see* **6** below).

(*b*) Without continuous stationery a large number of modern office machines would be unusable.

(*c*) Punched-card tabulators and computers work at too great a speed for separate forms to be continuously fed into the machine.

(*d*) Continuous stationery is also a method of obtaining several copies of a document simultaneously, which can be very useful, e.g. for sales invoicing.

4. Kinds of continuous stationery.

(*a*) *Roll stationery*, i.e. in a continuous roll, as on a teleprinter (not a very popular form).

(*b*) *Interfold*, where the stationery is folded flat in a "zig-zag" fashion (the most popular form).

(*c*) *Fanfold*, where the forms are not only joined end to end, but also horizontally and folded "concertina" fashion. If opened out the stationery would resemble a fan. This type is useful where it is wished to incorporate forms of different widths in one set, or where sprocket holes are not desired (*see* **5** below) and, perhaps, pre-punching is used for filing purposes.

5. Sprocket feeding.

(*a*) Both sides of the continuous stationery are punched with evenly spaced holes.

(*b*) The forms are controlled on a special platen assembly fitted with sprockets (wheels with protruding pins).

(*c*) The purpose is to ensure that the forms are held rigid and in good alignment.

(*d*) It prevents forms slipping out of position when in the machine.

6. Advantages of continuous stationery.

(*a*) It saves time used in feeding separate forms into a type-writer, tabulator, etc.

(*b*) It saves time in inserting (one-time carbon) and removing carbons (NCR and carbon backing).

(*c*) It facilitates the speedy use of accounting machines, addressing machines, etc.

NOTE: The average amount of typists' time saved is about 50 per cent, but with a twelve-part set and only five lines of typing on each form, as much as 78 per cent of a typist's time is saved. The time saved will be greater with an increase in the number of copies in a "set" and reduce with an increase in the average amount of typing on each form.

7. Disadvantages of continuous stationery.

(*a*) Difficulty (and expense) of obtaining skilled typists.

(*b*) Carbon copies are often smeared and dirty, and the last copies in a set sometimes indistinct and difficult to read.

(*c*) Continuous stationery is expensive and delivery may be slow if it is out of stock.

(*d*) When mistakes are made because of (*a*), it is difficult to rectify them and will be expensive in stationery.

NOTE: Many business concerns are today using alternative methods for obtaining various copies of documents, such as photocopying, addressing machines, spirit duplicating, etc.: *see* XVIII.

8. Uses of continuous stationery.

(*a*) Sales invoice sets, by which various copies are obtained for the accounts department, transport department, warehouse, sales representatives, etc.

(*b*) Order sets, consisting of:
   (*i*) one copy for the supplier;
   (*ii*) one for the buying department;
   (*iii*) one for the stores department, etc.

(*c*) Production of cheques where a large number are required.

(*d*) Wages preparation:
   (*i*) the pay-roll itself;
   (*ii*) pay statements;
   (*iii*) and even pay-envelopes are produced in continuous stationery form.

(*e*) Share registrar's department:
   (*i*) for acknowledgment of receipt of share transfer;
   (*ii*) notification to share registrar's clerk;
   (*iii*) copy to new certificate clerk, etc.

9. Snap carbon sets.

Where the volume of work does not justify the purchase of continuous stationery, sets of forms with inter-leaved carbons can be obtained which are lightly gummed along the tops of the forms. Individual sets are fed into the typewriter, etc., thereby saving the insertion of carbon and lining up of forms.

10. The impact of word-processing and microprocessors. The rapid development of these techniques will render obsolete many of the types of stationery described in this chapter, although they may continue in use for some years in smaller, non-automated offices.

A notable feature of the word-processing unit is its ability to produce as many perfect, error-free copies of letters, invoices, reports, etc., as may be required, while there is considerable economy in the use of paper generally: it is not necessary, for example, to retain carbon copies, since the material is in store and available for instant retrieval on the visual display screen.

Consequently, paper manufacturers must adapt to the changing demands for stationery.

PROGRESS TEST 17

1. What methods of copying are used in connection with continuous stationery? **(2)**

2. Compare and contrast interfold and fanfold stationery. **(4)**

3. What is the major purpose of sprocket feeding in the context of continuous stationery? **(5)**

4. State the two advantages and two disadvantages of continuous stationery which, in your opinion, are the most important. **(6, 7)**

5. Name six departments where it would be advantageous to use continuous stationery. **(8)**

6. Continuous stationery is too expensive for small companies, with a limited office output: what useful alternative is available between continuous and non-continuous stationery? **(9)**

CHAPTER XVIII

Duplicating and Office Printing

1. Definition. Duplicating is the name given to a process whereby a master copy is prepared from which a large number of other copies are automatically obtained.

The phenomenal growth in paperwork depends almost entirely on a ceaseless flow of forms, orders, invoices, stationery, multi-part sets, padded forms and cards. In many companies this wide range of printed material is now almost totally produced in the company's own print department, more usually known as the inplant print department. Some of the largest of these rival the largest commercial printers.

2. Different methods. The most commonly used methods are the stencil process, spirit duplicating, offset lithography and typeset lithography. Note that photocopying is not usually included as duplicating (*see* XIX, **9** and **10**).

3. Stencil process.

(*a*) With this method the master copy is a thin fibrous sheet covered with a plastic coating through which ink will not pass.

(*b*) The stencil is cut on a typewriter (or by a hand stylus) and placed on the outside of an inked drum on the machine.

(*c*) As the machine is operated, ink is forced through the cuts in the stencil, producing the image required on absorbent paper.

(*d*) Unless absorbent paper is used the ink will smudge and there is a danger of "offset" on to other sheets.

(*e*) Good quality stencils can produce as many as 5000 copies.

(*f*) The stencils can be stored and used again.

4. Electronic stencil.

(*a*) An important development has been the introduction of an electronic stencil machine which can photographically cut a stencil to the image required.

(*b*) This enables half-tone photographs, printed documents, etc., to be reproduced on an ordinary stencil duplicator.

(*c*) Although more expensive than the ordinary kind, electronic stencils are cheaper than printing.

5. Advantages and disadvantages of the stencil process.

(*a*) *Advantages.*

(*i*) Ease of altering the stencil (by use of correcting fluid).

(*ii*) Length of run, i.e. number of copies, obtainable from each stencil.

(*iii*) Good quality reproduction.

(*iv*) Photographic reproduction with electronic stencils.

(*v*) Stencils can be stored and used again.

(*vi*) Cheapness of copy paper.

(*b*) *Disadvantages.*

(*i*) Difficulty of registration where two or more colours are required.

(*ii*) Separate runs are required for two or more colours.

(*iii*) The absorbent quality of the copy paper.

(*iv*) Cost of stencils if only a few copies are required.

6. Applications of the stencil process. The stencil method of duplicating is suitable for any office job where several hundred or even a thousand or more copies are required, where good quality reproduction is wanted, and in particular, for:

(*a*) minutes of meetings (good quality);

(*b*) sales literature (with photographs);

(*c*) price lists (length of run);

(*d*) special circular letters to customers or shareholders (length of run).

7. Spirit duplicating.

(*a*) In this process the master copy is a piece of art paper (glossy on one side), prepared by typing or writing on it while backed with a piece of special hectorgraphic carbon paper.

(*b*) This creates a reverse image in carbon on the back of the paper.

(*c*) When the master copy is placed round a drum on the machine and the machine is operated, the copy paper is dampened with spirit so that some of the carbon is dissolved, leaving a positive image on the copy paper.

(*d*) About 100 to 200 copies can be obtained from each master copy before it is exhausted.

(*e*) As many as seven colours can be obtained on the master copy, and copied simultaneously, by the consecutive use of different coloured carbons.

(*f*) Good quality smooth-surfaced paper is best for use as copy paper.

NOTE: A selective spirit duplicator is obtainable by which selected material can be duplicated from a long list of items on the master copy. This is useful for production control and for export documentation.

8. Advantages and disadvantages of spirit duplicating.

(a) *Advantages.*

(i) Cheapness of both carbon and master paper.

(ii) Ease of preparing the master copy (e.g. it can be written with a ball-pen).

(iii) It is the only method by which many colours can be duplicated *simultaneously.*

(iv) Simplicity of preparation.

(v) Good quality paper is used for copies.

(b) *Disadvantages.*

(i) The image becomes progressively weaker as the carbon deposit is used up.

(ii) Difficulty of altering the master copy if mistakes are made.

(iii) Limited number of copies from each master.

(iv) Quality of reproduction is not as good as that from a stencil.

(v) Tends to stain the fingers.

9. Applications of spirit process. Spirit duplicating is suitable for any office job where only a few copies are required and where different colours might also be wanted and in particular for:

(a) sales invoicing (even for as few as six copies it may be preferable to continuous stationery);

(b) internal office circulars and notices;

(c) coloured charts and drawings;

(d) production control, for various copies of control documents.

10. Offset lithography. This is really a printing process.

(a) The basic principle relies on the antipathy of grease and water.

(b) The master copy is a metal plate photographically prepared.

(c) When it is placed on the machine it comes in contact with greasy ink and water, and the positive image is "offset" or transferred to a rubber-covered roller, giving a negative image.

(d) When paper is fed between this roller and an impression roller it receives the final positive image.

(*e*) Almost any paper can be used for copy paper (although proper printing papers are best).

(*f*) Separate runs have to be made with different plates for different colours.

(*g*) A paper plate costing only a few pence can be typed, using a special greasy inked ribbon, from which a thousand or more copies can be obtained. This gives a cheap form of duplicating.

(*h*) Paper plates can also be photographically prepared on some photocopying machines.

(*i*) As it is really a printing process, an offset lithography machine would not be purchased unless office printing was intended but, once installed, it presents a cheap form of duplicating.

11. Advantages and disadvantages of offset lithography.

(*a*) *Advantages*.

    (*i*) It is a cheap form of printing.

    (*ii*) The quality of reproduction is best of all.

    (*iii*) Any paper can be used.

    (*iv*) It reproduces photographically.

    (*v*) Length of run (50,000 or more can be obtained from a metal plate).

    (*vi*) Convenience to the management (particularly when a printed form is suddenly found to be out of stock).

(*b*) *Disadvantages*.

    (*i*) Separate runs are required for different colours.

    (*ii*) A trained operator is required—rather more so than for stencil or spirit duplicators.

    (*iii*) It is more expensive in capital outlay.

    (*iv*) It requires a great deal of office space for chemicals, plate and paper storage, etc., and this may involve additional security problems and insurance premiums.

12. Applications of offset lithography. It can be used for any office job where a printed appearance is required, and where long runs of many thousands may be wanted. It is particularly useful for:

(*a*) sales leaflets;

(*b*) staff magazines;

(*c*) internal office forms;

(*d*) catalogues (with photographs of products, etc.).

13. Typeset lithography. The master copy, in this process, consists of raised type arranged in channels round a drum on the machine, and printing is through an inked ribbon. The process is less popular in business than the three above.

(a) *Advantages.*
    (i) Reproduction of typewritten appearance can be obtained.
    (ii) Raised type printing is often of better quality than offset litho.
(b) *Disadvantages.*
    (i) Setting the type up is rather slow and laborious.
    (ii) Relatively expensive.

14. Applications of typeset lithography.

(a) Where facsimile typed letters are required.
(b) Where printing is required on card.

15. Choosing a duplicator. The main factors to be considered when choosing a machine are:

(a) frequency of use;
(b) the number of copies required from each master copy;
(c) capital outlay and running costs;
(d) simplicity in use;
(e) whether several colours are required;
(f) whether photographic reproduction is required (e.g. of half-tone photographs);
(g) durability and constancy of the image on all copies;
(h) quality of reproduction (e.g. is a printed appearance desirable?);
(i) ease of preparing the master copy;
(j) ease of correcting the master copy;
(k) availability of operators.

16. Other methods of duplicating. Note that an automatic typewriter can also be used to obtain many copies of a typewritten document.

17. Setting up an inplant department. Inplant does not operate on the same lines as a commercial printer. The latter costs each job not only to take account of anticipated idle time but also a level of profit. On the other hand, a company's inplant department costs each job to the client on the basis of prime cost, depreciation and other overheads. Idle time is total loss to the company, and therefore a major requirement when planning inplant printing is that the department shall be kept busy all the time. A rigorous O & M exercise should examine:

(a) all the company's printed forms and stationery in current and anticipated use;

(b) what part of them shall be done by the company; and what part shall be put out to commercial printers (the advantages of putting some portion of work out are to obtain useful standards by which to judge the company's own cost competitiveness and quality);

(c) what extra print is likely to be generated simply by having the print facility available;

(d) what are the expected quality standards;

(e) what is the maximum size of material to be printed. In this context A4 is usually chosen for both its fit on the small offset press and its place in the company's own paperwork based on international sizes.

18. Plain paper copying. In few other industries has a new technology turned the market around in so short a time. It is estimated that the production share lost by offset duplicators in 1977 alone is estimated to be 75 billion copies.

Cost reduction, convenience, new equipment and the continuing need for paper records justify the continued growth of office copying, in particular that of plain paper copying. Cost per copy has declined both absolutely and relatively. Plain paper costs on average only 20 per cent of the cost of coated paper.

Currently, plain paper machines are economic only for volumes in excess of 4000 per month. Capital costs are, however, higher than for conventional coated-copy machines, although competition among the many suppliers in the UK market should keep prices at a realistic level.

19. The impact of word-processing and microprocessing. The ability of these new techniques to produce as many copies as may be required introduces an extra dimension into the whole field of copying and duplicating. The fully automated office may well decide to dispense with many of the machines described in this chapter. Cost of production per copy must necessarily be the criterion.

PROGRESS TEST 18

1. What is an inplant printing department? **(1)**
2. For what type of output is spirit duplicating suitable? **(7)**
3. What is offset lithography and what are its advantages and disadvantages? **(10, 11)**
4. What are the major criteria for choosing a duplicator? **(15)**

5. What especial problems are involved when setting up an inplant printing department? **(17)**

6. To what do you attribute the remarkable decline in the use of offset duplicators? **(18, 19)**

CHAPTER XIX

Photocopying

1. Definition. Photocopying is a method of copying a document with photographic detail, and is generally used for obtaining one or at most a few copies of such documents.

The method used with most photocopying machines is "contact printing", where the original is exposed to light (or heat) with special light-sensitive (or heat-sensitive) paper.

The modern photocopier allows copies to be made under ordinary office lighting without the need for a dark room, running water, etc. Reference should be made to XVIII **18** and **19** in considering the effect of important recent techniques on photocopying.

2. Summary of methods.

    (*a*) Reflex.
    (*b*) Transfer diffusion.*
    (*c*) Gelatine transfer.
    (*d*) Direct positive.
    (*e*) Dyeline.*
    (*f*) Thermal process.*
    (*g*) Electrostatic.*
    (*h*) Pressure fixed dry-toned.

* These are probably the most popular methods in use, and should at least be known to the student of office administration.

3. Reflex photocopying. This process copies any kind of document, either opaque or translucent.

    (*a*) The method is nearest to ordinary photography.

    (*b*) A negative is created by exposing the original to light, after which any number of positive prints can be made by further exposure of the negative and a fresh positive paper.

    (*c*) Usually, two baths of chemicals are used for developing and fixing.

    (*d*) Very high quality copies are obtained.

    (*e*) *Advantages.*

        (*i*) It gives the best quality reproduction.

(*ii*) The negative will give an unlimited number of copies and can be stored for future use.

(*iii*) It will copy any type of document even if it is in colour (though the colours will be rendered in black and white).

(*f*) *Disadvantages.*

(*i*) It uses wet chemicals.

(*ii*) It is relatively expensive.

(*iii*) It is very sensitive to direct daylight.

4. Transfer diffusion. This was until recently a popular type of machine in use, and it is the cheapest.

(*a*) Usually the original is fed into the machine sandwiched between a piece of negative and a piece of positive paper.

(*b*) After exposure to light the original is removed.

(*c*) Negative and positive go through a combined developer and fixer.

(*d*) Finally the negative and positive are peeled apart, when the image will have been transferred from the negative to the positive paper.

(*e*) *Advantages.*

(*i*) Very good quality reproduction.

(*ii*) Any document in colour can be copied (but *see* **3**(*e*)(*iii*) above).

(*iii*) It can be used to create offset-litho plates.

(*iv*) Translucent masters can be created for further copy by dyeline.

(*f*) *Disadvantages.*

(*i*) It uses wet chemicals.

(*ii*) Negatives are re-usable but not so easily as in the reflex method.

(*iii*) Also sensitive to direct daylight.

5. Gelatine transfer. With this method the negative, called a "matrix", is coated with gelatine, from which a number of positives can be obtained.

(*a*) It uses an uncoated non-light sensitive copy paper and is therefore very cheap.

(*b*) As many as 15 copies can be obtained from one matrix, although their quality is not as good as with the reflex or transfer diffusion methods.

(*c*) *Advantages.*

(*i*) Cheap when several copies are required.

(*ii*) Offset-litho masters can be made on it.

(*iii*) It can copy any document and any colour.

(*d*) *Disadvantages.*

(*i*) The image is not as good as with the previously described procedures.

(*ii*) Matrices cannot be stored and used again.

(*iii*) The chemical solution needs to be at a certain temperature for good results.

6. Direct positive. This method has the advantage of operating (if necessary) without the use of a negative.

(*a*) The first exposure yields a black image on white ground, by the use of special translucent paper for the originals.

(*b*) If the original is not translucent, a negative copy is obtained.

(*c*) The sensitised materials used are less sensitive to light than those in the above processes.

(*d*) *Advantages.*

(*i*) Translucent copies can be made direct.

(*ii*) It copies any document and any colour.

(*e*) *Disadvantage.* A reversed or translucent copy is not always acceptable.

7. Dyeline (or diazo). The originals, in this process, need to be on transparent or translucent paper.

(*a*) The method consists of placing the original in contact with special dyeline paper and exposing it to light (no negative is employed).

(*b*) The light bleaches the paper white except where the image occurs.

(*c*) The image is then fixed by chemical fumes or wet chemicals.

(*d*) *Advantages.*

(*i*) It is the cheapest method of photocopying.

(*ii*) It can be used in ordinary daylight.

(*iii*) It has a wide range of applications in the office.

(*iv*) The originals can be stored and used again.

(*e*) *Disadvantages.*

(*i*) Originals need to be translucent or transparent and single-sided only.

(*ii*) Not such good quality reproduction.

8. Thermal. Here the equipment contains an infra-red lamp which emits heat.

(*a*) The original is fed into the machine along with a piece of special heat-sensitive paper.

(b) A copy is then automatically produced without wet chemicals at all, and in a matter of seconds.

(c) The ink on the original needs to have a carbon content or it will not copy it; thus ordinary ball-pen ink does not reproduce, although special "reproduction" ball-pens can be obtained which will copy.

(d) *Advantages.*

(i) The fastest method of all (four seconds).

(ii) Completely dry; no wet chemicals are used.

(iii) Spirit-duplicating masters can be made on it photographically.

(iv) Very simple to operate.

(e) *Disadvantages.*

(i) Heat-sensitive paper does not give a very good quality image (although one machine produces better quality copies obtainable with heat-sensitive carbons on ordinary paper).

(ii) It only copies originals the ink of which has a carbon content.

(iii) Some colours (red, green, etc.) will not copy at all.

9 Electrostatic.

(a) On an electrostatic machine the image from the original is projected on to a selenium-coated plate charged with electricity.

(b) Powdered ink, also charged with electricity, is showered over the plate and when ordinary paper is placed into contact with the plate the ink adheres to it.

(c) The ink is then fused on the paper by the application of heat.

(d) *Advantages.*

(i) No wet chemicals are involved.

(ii) It uses ordinary paper.

(iii) Good quality reproduction.

(iv) An unlimited number of copies of the original are obtainable.

(e) *Disadvantages.*

(i) It is suitable only for a large volume of work (machines are usually supplied on rental basis).

(ii) Sometimes repeated maintenance is required.

(iii) It will not copy all colours equally well.

(iv) With a large volume of work the selenium drum has to be replaced at intervals, and the quality of the image fades.

(f) Electrostatic machines are now available which will produce continuous copies of a document, and which are being marketed as duplicators. Being simple to operate and providing good quality

copies, there is a great temptation to use such machines as duplicators, i.e. for long runs, but although very convenient, it is
doubtful if they are as economical as stencil or spirit duplicators,
i.e. if copy has to be typed anyway.

10. Pressure fixed dry-toned copiers. This is a recent UK development suitable for the low to medium volume market (2500 to
6000 copies a month) requiring high quality reproduction.

(*a*) Cost of the copies is substantially lower than plain paper.

(*b*) The copies produced are akin to those on plain paper, but
with added quality. This is very apparent in copying pictures, half-
tones, heavy type and solid areas.

(*c*) During the process the toner powder used by the copier is
fused under pressure to the paper (*see* **9**).

11. Advantages of photocopying.

(*a*) Exact facsimile copies are obtained of every detail.

(*b*) When only a few copies are required it is the cheapest form
of duplicating.

(*c*) It obviates the need for checking.

(*d*) It is useful when the number of copies required varies.

(*e*) It can be operated by a junior (e.g. compared with a skilled
typist if there is no photocopier).

(*f*) Reduction or enlargement of image is available on many
copiers.

12. Disadvantages of photocopying.

(*a*) Photocopies tend to fade, although a great deal depends on
the quality of the processing; the electrostatic method is probably
best on this score.

(*b*) Photocopy paper (where used) tends to curl, making filing
difficult.

(*c*) It may be expensive when a number of copies are required.

(*d*) Some machines do not copy colours or ball-pen ink.

(*e*) Difficulty of setting exposure times accurately, thus leading
to a waste of materials.

(*f*) Corrosion of the machine and the wasting property of wet
chemicals (where used). In some modern machines the chemicals
are stored in plastic bags to prevent either happening.

13. Uses of photocopying.

(*a*) Incoming letters for the attention of different departments
(no delay in distribution of copies).

(b) Copying complicated documents which can be lodged with the bank, e.g. insurance policies and contracts, etc.

(c) Sales invoice systems; a systems machine is obtainable which reproduces the same information on different documents with different headings.

(d) In the accountant's department, for obtaining monthly statements by photocopying the sales ledger cards.

(e) In the share registrar's department for retaining copies of death certificates, probate, letters of administration, etc.

(f) For supplying sales representatives with up-to-date copies of lists of the customers in their areas from a master index kept at head office.

(g) For copying hand-drawn charts, graphs, etc.

14. Buying a photocopier. A photocopying machine should be bought which is most suitable for the purposes for which it is to be used and these factors should be considered:

(a) The number of copies of each document required.

(b) The size of the originals.

(c) Whether the original is opaque or translucent.

(d) Whether the original is double or single sided.

(e) Speed of reproduction.

(f) Are the originals in colour?

(g) Is ball-pen writing to be copied?

(h) Ease and simplicity of operation.

(i) Liquid chemicals or a dry process?

(j) Quality of reproduction.

(k) Permanence of image (if required).

(l) Capital outlay and running costs.

(m) Can the master be stored and used again (if required)?

PROGRESS TEST 19

1. Examine the merits and demerits of transfer diffusion, diazo and thermal photocopying. **(4, 7, 8)**

2. In general, copying is understood to mean the production of only a few copies of a document: which copying devices are available for use as duplicators for long runs? **(9, 10)**

3. Is a high degree of skill, and therefore, training required in operating photocopying devices? **(10)**

4. What are the major disadvantages of photocopying? **(12)**

5. What are the major uses of photocopying? **(13)**

6. What major criteria would influence you in buying a photocopier? **(14)**

CHAPTER XX

Addressing Machines

1. Definition. An addressing machine is an office machine which duplicates information from masters but, instead of producing many copies from one master only, it prints one copy or a few of each of a series of masters.

It is a most useful machine when it is wished to duplicate standard information at regular intervals. "Addressing" comes from the original purpose for which the machine was devised—the duplicating of a series of names and addresses—but many other uses are made of the machine today.

The three main kinds of addressing machine are listed below.

2. Embossed metal plates. These print through an inked ribbon.

   (*a*) *Advantages.*
   (*i*) Plates are more durable.
   (*ii*) Best where carbon copies are required.
   (*iii*) Machines are highly developed, being the first type to be introduced.
   (*iv*) A good quality image is obtainable.
   (*b*) *Disadvantages.*
   (*i*) The plates are very heavy to carry about.
   (*ii*) Delay in embossing, unless an embossing machine is purchased (extra expense).
   (*iii*) Noisy.

3. Stencil frames. These can be cut by the use of a special fitment on the platen of a typewriter.

   (*a*) The principle of reproduction is the same as with a stencil duplicator.
   (*b*) *Advantages.*
   (*i*) Stencils are lighter in weight.
   (*ii*) Stencils are easily prepared.
   (*iii*) Less noisy than a plate machine.
   (*iv*) Stencils are cheaper than metal plates.
   (*c*) *Disadvantages.*

(*i*) Quality of reproduction is not so good as with a metal plate machine.

(*ii*) Rather dirty process.

(*iii*) Not as durable as metal plates.

4. Spirit process machine. The master copies are of glossy paper and made with hectographic carbon paper in the same way that spirit duplicator masters are made.

(*a*) The master copies are in cardboard or plastic frames and the surface of the copy paper is first dampened with spirit before printing.

(*b*) *Advantages*.

(*i*) Light in weight.

(*ii*) Ease of preparing master copies.

(*iii*) Cheaper even than stencils.

(*iv*) Different colours can be produced simultaneously.

(*c*) *Disadvantages*.

(*i*) Quality of printing not as good as with the methods described above.

(*ii*) Other disadvantages of spirit duplicating (*see* XVIII, **9**).

5. Operational features. A simple hand-operated addressing machine will be different in operation from a large, expensive, electrically-driven machine, but in general they include the following operational features:

(*a*) Automatic feed and ejection of plates and/or forms.

(*b*) "Cut-out" or masking device, where only part of the information on a plate is to be printed, e.g. any line(s) to the exclusion of the other lines.

(*c*) If required, they will print the master copies in a continuous list on a sheet of paper instead of on separate forms.

(*d*) A duplex listing machine will print alternately from left to right.

(*e*) Automatic selection, by means of signals on the addressing media, and a selection device which will print only those masters with signals in a certain position on the plates, etc.

(*f*) Facilities for adding variable information for a special run, e.g. "Private and confidential".

(*g*) Repeating device by which each plate can be repeated automatically on the machine.

(*h*) "Skip" mechanism by which unwanted plates can be omitted from the printing sequence.

(*i*) Numbering device for numbering each impression with the same number or a consecutive number each time.

(*j*) Attachment for facsimile writing and signatures.

(*k*) Device for entering the date at each impression.

6. Advantages of addressing machines.

(*a*) Economy of time and effort.

(*b*) They are useful for repeat printing of any standing information, in place of typing.

(*c*) They can be operated by junior labour, instead of skilled typists.

(*d*) They obviate checking.

(*e*) Saving in staff and overhead expenses.

7. Disadvantages.

(*a*) Delay caused by sending plates away for embossing, i.e. if a metal plate machine is used and an embossing machine is not purchased.

(*b*) Unless a hard and fast system is used for amending the master copy list, it easily becomes out of date.

(*c*) Metal plate machine is very noisy.

NOTE: *See* **2–4** above for separate advantages and disadvantages of the various machines.

8. Uses of addressing machines.

(*a*) For heading up sales invoices and monthly statements.

(*b*) For producing dividend warrants and dividend lists (note the application of the repeat device on warrants in duplicate, and of the listing device for a dividend list).

(*c*) Different forms in connection with meetings: notices, agenda papers, proxies, etc.

(*d*) Preparation of the pay-roll (note the use of the masking device when only pay number, name and occupation may be required from the plate, excluding address, date of birth, etc.), for putting pay numbers on pay envelopes, time cards, etc.

(*e*) Heading up ledger cards. One machine (spirit process) has aperture ledger cards and the ledger card is then also a combined addressing medium.

(*f*) Various kinds of index lists: for credit ratings, address records, commission lists, etc.

(*g*) For producing various documents required in connection with production control, e.g. job card, material requisition, route card, etc.

(*h*) For credit control purposes: by issuing each customer with an embossed addressing plate (usually made of plastic), production of which is proof of credit account.

9. The impact of new techniques. If a list of names and addresses has been committed to the memory of the word-processing unit, a batch of standard letters, price-lists, etc., can be produced, each with its individual address. Each letter will be perfect: no operator need attend.

In the fully-automated office, therefore, many of the machines described in this chapter are not necessary: their use will continue for some years in the smaller, non-automated office.

PROGRESS TEST 20

1. In what important respect does an addressing machine differ from duplicating machines in general?   **(1)**

2. What kind of machine is suitable where a good quality image is the most important consideration? What disadvantages are there with this machine?   **(2)**

3. What are the major operational features common to simple hand-operated addressing machines and electrically driven machines?   **(5)**

4. List the major uses of addressing machines.   **(8)**

5. Is there any realistic alternative to addressing machines in the office of a medium-sized manufacturing company?   **(6)**

CHAPTER XXI

Adding and Calculating Machines

1. Adding machines. There are two main kinds of adding machine:

(*a*) *Listing/adding machine*, which gives a printed record of all figures put in the machine on a paper strip called a tally roll. Its advantages include:

    (*i*) it gives a printed record of amounts set up in the machine;

    (*ii*) this gives ease of checking figures put in the machine;

    (*iii*) credits are usually printed in red.

(*b*) *Non-listing adding machine*, which records the totals in dials on the machine only.

2. Types of keyboard. These are full-bank, half-keyboard and simplified keyboard.

(*a*) The *half-keyboard* type has keys numbered 1–5 for each digital position on the machine, and two keys have to be pressed consecutively for numbers over 5. This type of keyboard is really a cheaper and lighter (in weight) version of the full-bank keyboard.

    (*i*) Touch operation easier to learn.

    (*ii*) Compact machine and lighter in weight.

    (*iii*) Less hand travel; faster.

(*b*) *Full-bank and simplified keyboards* are also provided for calculating and accounting machines. The full-bank has keys numbered 1–9 for each digital position on the machine, whereas the simplified keyboard has ten keys only numbered 0 and 1–9.

    (*i*) Simultaneous entry of figures is possible.

    (*ii*) Visible check on entry before the machine is operated.

    (*iii*) Noughts are printed automatically.

    (*iv*) Figures on keyboard (£ p) are easy to identify.

3. Operational features of adding machines. The following mechanical features are obtainable on adding machines:

    (*a*) Non-print key (when a printed record is not required).

    (*b*) Addition and subtraction keys.

    (*c*) Total and sub-total keys.

    (*d*) Credit balances printed in red.

    (*e*) Repeat key when it is wished to repeat an item *ad lib*.

(*f*) Non-add key, when a straight list only is required.

(*g*) Dials showing digits entered on the machine.

Adding machines can be manually or electrically operated.

4. Uses of adding machines.

(*a*) Cross-casting is faster and easier (unnecessary to have figures in rigid vertical columns).

(*b*) Adding cheques received in the post.

(*c*) Checking addition in ledgers.

(*d*) Adding columns of figures on pay-roll.

(*e*) Pre-listing sales invoices before posting.

5. Calculating machines. While the main functions of *adding* machines are addition and subtraction, *calculating* machines are basically for multiplication and division, although addition and subtraction can also be performed on them.

6. Calculating without machines. Machines are not always advisable, and the following methods (*see* **7–9**) should be considered before buying a machine.

7. Mental calculation.

(*a*) *Advantages*.

    (*i*) No expensive machine.

    (*ii*) Speedy, if calculations are simple.

    (*iii*) Sufficient for occasional calculations.

    (*iv*) Part of clerical training.

    (*v*) The retention of skill in mental calculation is a powerful corrective to the risk of degenerating into a "slave of the machine".

(*b*) *Disadvantages*.

    (*i*) Tiring if frequent.

    (*ii*) May be slow.

    (*iii*) May be incorrect.

8. Ready reckoner.

(*a*) *Advantages*.

    (*i*) Simple and easy to use.

    (*ii*) Cheap to buy.

    (*iii*) Suitable for simple calculations.

(*b*) *Disadvantages*.

    (*i*) May be slow.

    (*ii*) Possibility of misreading.

    (*iii*) Not always suitable.

9. Slide rule.

(*a*) *Advantages.*

(*i*) Cheap and portable.

(*ii*) Good for approximations.

(*iii*) Although addition and subtraction cannot be performed, multiplication and division, involution and evolution, trigonometrical calculations, etc., can be performed on the "scholar" or "universal" type of slide rule. In the hands of an expert the relative percentage error of the slide rule is very small.

(*b*) *Disadvantages.*

(*i*) Insufficient accuracy where precision is required.

(*ii*) Some training is necessary, and plenty of practice.

10. Calculating machines. These include:

(*a*) printing calculator;

(*b*) key-driven calculator;

(*c*) rotary calculator;

(*d*) electric automatic machine; and

(*e*) electronic calculator.

11. Printing calculator. This machine has developed from an adding/listing machine, usually with a simplified keyboard.

(*a*) Machines are available with double registers and memory register.

(*b*) Calculations are made simply by setting up the figures required and then pressing the appropriate multiplication or division key, and the answer is printed automatically on a tally-roll.

(*c*) It is electrically operated.

(*d*) *Advantages.*

(*i*) Simple in operation (no trained operator required).

(*ii*) Gives a visual check of figures set up.

(*iii*) Chain discount calculations are simplified.

(*e*) *Disadvantages.*

(*i*) Can be relatively slow.

(*ii*) More expensive than some calculating machines.

12. Key-driven calculator. This machine has a full-bank keyboard, and when the keys are depressed the answers are shown on dials on the machine.

(*a*) Multiplication is really repeated addition and division really repeated subtraction.

(*b*) It works in decimals only.

(*c*) *Advantages.*

(*i*) Great speed.

(*ii*) Suitable for a large volume of work.

(*d*) *Disadvantages*.

(*i*) Trained operator required.

(*ii*) Since no visual check of figures is put into the calculator, accuracy must be verified either by repeating the calculation, or, preferably, by the use of check figures (*see* XXXVI).

13. Rotary calculator. This kind of calculator can be lever-set or key-set.

(*a*) Calculations are performed by turning a handle—clockwise for multiplication and anti-clockwise for division.

(*b*) It has a manually operated carriage shift for moving the decimal place.

(*c*) *Advantages*.

(*i*) Light and portable.

(*ii*) Simple to operate.

(*iii*) Sufficiently fast for general purposes.

(*d*) *Disadvantage*. No record of calculations.

14. Electric automatic calculator. This machine is a development of the rotary calculator, but is powered by an electric motor.

(*a*) There are separate sections on the keyboard for multiplicand and multiplier.

(*b*) On depressing the keys it performs calculations automatically, showing the answers in dials on the machine.

(*c*) *Advantages*.

(*i*) Greater speed than previous machines.

(*ii*) It is fully automatic.

(*iii*) Fairly simple to operate.

(*d*) *Disadvantages*.

(*i*) Not very portable.

(*ii*) Relatively expensive.

(*iii*) Relatively noisy.

15. Electronic calculator. This machine is similar in operation to a key-driven calculator.

(*a*) The answers are shown in lighted figures in dials.

(*b*) The calculations are performed electronically instead of mechanically.

(*c*) *Advantages*.

(*i*) Great speed.

(*ii*) It is fully automatic.

(*iii*) Quiet in operation.

(*d*) *Disadvantage*. Relatively expensive.

16. Electronic printing calculator. This machine is similar to the electric printing calculator except that it works electronically, i.e. is very fast and very quiet, but gives a printed record (print-out) of the calculations.

17. Programmable electronic calculator. This is a development of the electronic printing calculator.

(*a*) It is half-way to being a computer, in so far as it performs calculations automatically in accordance with a standard programme.

(*b*) Only variables in the calculation need to be set in the machine.

(*c*) The various programmes can be set manually into the machine or fed in on magnetic striped cards, or by edge-punched cards.

(*d*) A recent development is the pocket programmable calculator, costing under £20 in 1978. In conjunction with its programme library, it combines a variety of specialist calculators: financial, statistical, mathematical, engineering, etc. Input is achieved simply by pressing keys.

18. Factors in choice of a calculating machine.

(*a*) Type of calculation required.

(*b*) Number of digits, i.e. figures to be put into the machine, as well as in the answer.

(*c*) Speed required.

(*d*) Simplicity of operation (is a trained operator required?).

(*e*) Volume and frequency of calculations.

(*f*) Capital outlay.

(*g*) Size and portability of machine.

(*h*) Degree of accuracy required.

(*i*) Is a printed record of calculations required?

(*j*) Are the calculations lengthy and of a standard nature?

19. New techniques. The rapid development of the "silicon chip" and the vast field of microprocessor systems inevitably render most of the machines described here obsolete, although their use will continue for some years in small, non-automated offices.

PROGRESS TEST 21

1. Describe the operational features of adding machines. **(3)**

2. Examine the arguments in favour of the slide-rule. **(9)**

3. A routine calculation in a sales-invoice department is the adjustment of the catalogue price by several discounts, both added to and subtracted from the preceding result. Describe the most suitable non-electronic calculator. **(11)**

4. What are the basic differences between a key-driven, a rotary and a printing calculator? **(11–13)**

5. Assuming additional cost to be relatively unimportant, what major considerations would lead you to prefer the electronic to the non-electronic type of calculator? **(15–17)**

6. Is the lack of trained staff, in your opinion, a deterrent to the purchase of calculating equipment? **(Passim)**

CHAPTER XXII

Accounting Machines

1. Definition. Accounting machines are electrically operated, and used primarily for posting to ledger accounts.

(*a*) They may be fitted with a number of adding registers for analysis purposes.

(*b*) They may have special keyboard facilities for entering details when posting.

(*c*) They usually have a special front-feed device to give speed when feeding ledger cards to the machine (note that billing, or invoicing, or book-keeping machines are all included under this heading).

2. Types of accounting machine. Accounting machines can be divided into those with:

(*a*) simplified keyboards (*see* XXI, **2**) or
(*b*) full-bank keyboards.

For the purpose of entering details when posting, machines can also be divided into:

(*c*) those which print the invoice number only (cheapest);
(*d*) those with limited description (or symbol) keys (slightly dearer);
(*e*) those with full typewriter keyboards, for typing full details when posting.

3. Operational features. Accounting machines depend on the use of loose-leaf ledgers and the entering of two or more documents simultaneously.

The various mechanical features to be obtained on different machines include:

(*a*) automatic movement of the carriage after each entry, perhaps with automatic repeat printing;

(*b*) automatic calculation and printing of new account balance at each entry;

(*c*) if the machine is fitted with a memory or cumulating register, automatic totalling of all entries made to different accounts;

(d) automatic printing of the date when the details are entered;

(e) a number of adding registers, which enables multiple analyses to be made;

(f) split platen, by which two documents move at different speeds through the machine;

(g) ordinary back feed, and front feed for ledger cards;

(h) the more expensive machines have programme bars or control bars which automatically convert the machines for different purposes.

4. Mechanised accounting technique. Since the posting of the sales ledger is a voluminous business and the most popular application of accounting machines, the following is an outline of their use:

(a) Total the invoices to be posted (pre-listing).

(b) Prepare ledger cards by
  (i) off-setting,
  (ii) stuffing invoices in between ledger cards in posting tray, or
  (iii) extracting appropriate ledger cards. Possibly monthly statements will also be prepared simultaneously and paired with the ledger cards.

(c) As each invoice is posted, "pick-up" the previous balance and check at the final stage (perhaps repeat the pick-up).

(d) As ledger cards are posted, a carbon copy of each posting will be obtained on a summary or proof sheet.

(e) At the end of a batch of posting (e.g. all sales invoices, but credits are posted separately), compare the total on the proof sheet with the pre-list (proof of accuracy).

(f) If they are in agreement, post this total to the appropriate control account.

5. Advantages of accounting machines.

(a) Time and labour saved in posting (about four to six times faster than posting by hand).

(b) Greater legibility and neatness of entries.

(c) Greater accuracy (*see* **4**).

(d) Automatic calculation and printing of the new account balance at each posting.

(e) Simultaneous posting in one operation of the journal (or proof sheet), ledger and monthly statement is possible.

(f) More information to management and quicker than previously.

6. Disadvantages of accounting machines.

(a) In a medium-sized business two operators may have to be employed even though there is sufficient work for one only.

(b) Capital outlay on the machine up to £7000).

(c) Disadvantages of having ledgers on the loose-leaf system (leaves can be mislaid, misfiled, etc.).

(d) Sometimes lack of detail in statements, etc., produced (there may be invoice numbers only).

(e) Machine breakdown or power failure.

(f) Noise in the office.

(g) Difficulty of obtaining skilled operators.

7. Loose-leaf ledgers.
Section 436 of the Companies Act 1948, impliedly allows the use of a loose-leaf ledger in registered companies, provided "adequate precautions shall be taken for guarding against falsification and for facilitating its discovery".
The precautions include:

(a) the provision of locking devices to the loose-leaf binders, the key being in the charge of a responsible person;

(b) control over the issue of loose leaves, which should be numbered consecutively;

(c) any scrapped stationery must be sufficiently explained.

(d) *Bound books.*

   (i) Contain all the accounts, so they are not split up.

   (ii) Accounts cannot be lost or misfiled.

   (iii) Best for prevention of fraud.

   (iv) May be cheaper.

(e) *Loose-leaf.*

   (i) Dead accounts can be removed (always a live index of accounts).

   (ii) Accounts can be rearranged in any desired order.

   (iii) Can be posted on accounting machine or writing board.

   (iv) Signals can be used to denote credit ratings, etc.

   (v) No blank pages to turn over.

   (vi) Ledgers can be split up at audit time, and for convenience of working.

8. Uses of accounting machines.

(a) For posting the sales ledger, when the ledger card, statement and proof sheet can be entered simultaneously.

(b) For posting the purchase ledger, when the remittance advice, ledger card and proof sheet can be entered simultaneously.

(c) For cheque writing, when cheques (in continuous stationery form) and the credit side of the cash book are entered together.

(d) For receipt writing, when the entering of the receipt, the paying-in list to the bank and the debit side of the cash book are entered simultaneously.

(e) For the pay-roll, when the pay-roll, pay statements and earnings records can be entered simultaneously.

(f) For all other purposes where posting and analysis are required, e.g. stock records, costing, etc.

9. Factors to consider when buying an accounting machine.

(a) How much detail is required in posting ledgers, etc. (e.g. whether to have a typewriter keyboard or symbol keys).

(b) Whether a simplified figure keyboard or full-bank keyboard is required.

(c) The number of adding registers, which depends on the number of analysis headings required.

(d) Can the machine be converted for different uses (incidence of programme bar)?

(e) Capital outlay and the maintenance service provided.

(f) Mechanical features, such as a front feed device and an automatic line-feeding device.

(g) Ease of operation and inspecting work in machine.

(h) Noise in operation.

10. Writing boards.
These consist of hard plastic boards, with a clipping device on the left-hand side, on which several documents (e.g. ledger sheet, monthly statement and journal sheet) are entered simultaneously by means of interleaved carbons.

Special writing boards (sometimes called "three-in-one systems") are available for the writing of the pay-roll, whereby automatic alignment can be obtained for the entering of the pay-roll, statements of pay and the tax records.

(a) An adding machine is required, otherwise a writing board offers some of the facilities of an accounting machine.

(b) They are less expensive than accounting machines and are most suitable for the smaller business concern.

(c) Writing boards can be used for ledger posting, pay-roll work, or for any other office function involving the entering of several forms with the same information.

(d) No specially trained operators are required, and they save a great deal of labour in repeat copying.

11. Visible record computers. These are electronic accounting machines which have many of the characteristics of large-scale computers, viz.

(*a*) Speed of entry, being many times faster than an ordinary electro-mechanical machine.

(*b*) Automatic pick up of old balance when posting, by means of magnetic strips on the ledger cards.

(*c*) Automatic programming of the machine for different purposes, e.g. by means of different reels of magnetic tape.

(*d*) Where electro-mechanical machines usually only perform addition and subtraction, the VRCs will perform multiplication and division automatically according to the programme.

(*e*) Being electronic, the machines are much quieter than the older type of accounting machines.

(*f*) At the same time as posting ledgers, punched paper tape or magnetic tape can be automatically prepared for feeding to a computer.

(*g*) The machines can be used for creating sales invoices, as well as for ledger posting purposes.

(*h*) At the same time as posting, the machine can be programmed to perform sales analysis.

(*i*) *Advantages.*

(*i*) Greater speed than electro-mechanical machines.

(*ii*) Greater flexibility in use.

(*iii*) Compared with main frame computers, no expensive specialist staff is required.

(*iv*) The manufacturers produce the programming required.

(*v*) Comparatively short training of operators (a good typist can learn to operate a VRC in a few days).

(*vi*) Only a small capital outlay compared with a main frame computer.

(*vii*) Gives historical and up-to-date ledger accounts, for reference purposes. (Batch posting with large computers, often means delays in obtaining the current position of an account.)

(*j*) *Disadvantages.*

(*i*) Limited capacity of the programmes.

(*ii*) May be dearer than older types of electro-mechanical accounting machine.

(*iii*) More expensive stationery (magnetic stripping).

12. New techniques. The rapid advance of microprocessor systems adds a new dimension to mechanised accounting.

There is a wide choice of "software" to suit individual requirements:

(*a*) *Sales Accounting*. The Open Item format means that all outstanding transactions, including those from previous months, are held on file until they are cleared by cash, credit or transfer. The key advantage of this approach over the traditional *balance forward* system is the vast reduction of customer queries on previous balances, since each monthly statement quotes all outstanding items comprehensively with date and reference details). All data handled by the ledger can be automatically transferred to a "Database" for subsequent analysis; statistics on products, representatives, areas, budgets, etc., can be monitored.

(*b*) *Purchase Accounting*. Like Sales Accounting, the system uses the Open Item format. An "audit trail" ensures a permanent printed record of all items passing through the system. The conventional purchases day book is thereby replaced.

(*c*) *"Database"*. This module automatically transfers data from other modules such as the sales and purchase ledgers; data can be displayed on the video screen and full printed reports are available to individual specifications.

Clearly, these new techniques render obsolete many of the accounting machines described in this chapter. Their use, however, will continue in the non-automated office.

PROGRESS TEST 22

1. What major operational features may be obtained from the range of electro-mechanical machines available? (**3**)

2. Describe how you would prepare an accounting machine for a long "credit run" (purchases invoices). (**4**)

3. What are the major disadvantages of accounting machines? (**6**)

4. There is only qualified legal approval of loose-leaf ledgers. What risks are inherent in their use, and what adequate precautions should be taken? (**7**)

5. In addition to book-keeping entries, for what other purposes may accounting machines be used? (**8**)

6. You are being urged to buy an expensive accounting machine to replace an existing manual posting system. What major factors ought you to consider? (**9**)

7. What are VRCs and what are their major advantages? (**11**)

8. Explain how the use of mechanised book-keeping conduces to greater accuracy. (passim)

9. What documents are commonly entered simultaneously on accounting machines? (passim)

10. What is the Open Item format, and what is its importance? (12)

11. What is "Database"? (12)

CHAPTER XXIII

Analysis by Hand Methods

1. Introduction. A routine requirement in business is that of analysing a large volume of data into homogeneous groups, e.g.:

(*a*) analysis of total sales into departments, different products, by areas, by representatives, etc.;

(*b*) analysis of total pay-roll into flat-rate, overtime and production bonus, timekeeping bonus, etc.;

(*c*) analysis of personnel by sex, age, degree of skill, department, etc.

2. Methods. Excluding the use of punched card machines, the different methods include:

(*a*) The use of adding machines and the addition of items under the different heads of analysis until the batch of documents (e.g. sales invoices) is exhausted (sometimes called the "exhaust" method). The total of the sub-headings should then equal the total of the whole.

(*b*) Peg-board.

(*c*) Marginally punched cards (sometimes called "edge-punched").

(*d*) Slotted cards.

(*e*) Feature cards.

3. Peg-board. This is a rectangular plastic board with evenly spaced pegs along the top.

(*a*) Paper forms with similarly spaced holes along their tops are then hung on the pegs, so that each form overlaps another, revealing a line of information on each form to be analysed.

(*b*) A "cursor" slides up and down on the board by means of which it is easy to summarise the figures on the exposed edges of the forms, and cross-cast, either mentally or with an adding machine.

(*c*) This is a relatively inexpensive method, and the forms contain the actual figures returned.

(*d*) The use of the peg-board saves copying and checking the figures.

4. Marginal punched cards. This is the method whereby cards of any desired size have holes equally spaced along one or more edges of the cards, and where the different analysis headings are printed against the holes.

(*a*) Entries are written in the centre of the card, and the different holes are then slotted out with a hand-slotting machine to present the information to be analysed.

(*b*) When a number of cards have been slotted it is a simple job to sort out any particular group by merely passing a needle through the appropriate hole and lifting, when the required cards drop off the needle.

(*c*) To give analysis totals, an adding machine can then be used for each group as it is needle-sorted.

(*d*) No expensive machine is required (although *see* note below); the method is very flexible, for the card can be printed any desired size according to the volume of information to be analysed.

(*e*) It is speedy in sorting out, and visual checking of the slotting is possible when the information is entered in the body of the card.

NOTE: The Royal-McBee marginal punched system, now on sale in the UK, uses (if so desired) an electric slotting machine, and has an electric tabulator which interprets sterling amounts punched in the cards and totals them.

(*f*) Marginal punched cards are used for sales analysis, statistical analysis and even for analysis of accounts and the preparation of final accounts.

EXAMPLE

A company employs 1000 persons and a comprehensive analysis by sex, age (over and under 21) and department (A or B) is required quickly. The personnel office has 1000 marginal punched cards in alphabetical order of the employees' surnames, slotted at the margin to give the requisite data for each person. After seven needle-sortings the following data are derived:

Department A: Total 502,
of whom 117 are under 21, of whom 49 are women.

Department B: 84 women over 21

Total factory: Total 301 under 21,
of whom 97 are women.

Total women
over 21: 208

These 7 facts, together with the total of 1000 provide the 8 degrees of freedom which can then be inserted into Table V to derive the 19 constraints to provide, finally, the 27 different facts relating to the personnel.

TABLE V: Analysis of employees by department, sex and age.

	Department A			Department B			Total		
	M	F	total	M	F	total	M	F	total
Under 21	68	49	117	136	48	184	204	97	301
Over 21	261	124	385	230	84	314	491	208	699
Total	329	173	502	366	132	498	695	305	1000

Once the 8 degrees of freedom have been correctly written in the Table, the 19 constraints are derived by adding or subtracting, as required.

5. Slotted cards. This system uses standard-size cards (203 mm × 203 mm or 203 mm × 152 mm) with columns of equally spaced holes in the body of the cards.

(*a*) Printed analysis headings are placed over different columns or sections of columns according to the analysis required.

(*b*) Information is "entered" on the cards by means of a simple slotting punch which joins two holes together to form a slot in the appropriate position on the card.

(*c*) The cards are then placed in a "selector" or sorting box and rods are passed through holes in the end of the box according to the analysis desired.

(*d*) When the selector is inverted (it is suspended on a swivel) the cards which have been slotted in the position of the rod fall down the depth of the slot (about 10 mm).

(*e*) The selector is then turned the right way up, a lifting rod inserted in the cards offset, and the selector rod withdrawn. The cards are then totalled and analysed by adding machine if desired.

(*f*) As many as 800 cards can be sorted simultaneously by this method, and it is very popular for staff records.

6. Feature cards. With this system, each card represents a particular feature, quality or analysis head of a collection of data.

(*a*) Each card is ruled so that there is a pattern of small squares printed on the face, e.g. a card measuring 152 mm by 279 mm provides 1000 numbered positions.

(*b*) Thus, if staff statistics of a large company were being analysed, the 1000 numbered positions would represent pay numbers 1–1000 and each card would bear a heading: "Male", "Female", "Clerks", etc.

(*c*) By means of a simple hand-operated punch, holes are then punched over the appropriate numbers in each card.

(*d*) Thus, if it was wished to have a multiple analysis of the data on the cards, say of:

    (*i*) all clerks;

    (*ii*) those living in the London area; and

    (*iii*) those earning between £2500 and £5000 per annum, cards representing these three features would be placed on top of one another, and when they were held up to the light daylight would show through the numbered positions which were punched in identical places on the three cards, i.e. having the common characteristics.

(*e*) This method has been used for:

    (*i*) personnel records;

    (*ii*) medical research;

    (*iii*) library indexing;

    (*iv*) market research;

    (*v*) criminal records; and

    (*vi*) property records.

PROGRESS TEST 23

1. Give examples, preferably from your own experience, of analysis that can conveniently be done by hand methods. (**1**)

2. For what kinds of analysis is a peg-board convenient? (**3**)

3. What is the advantage of selecting the "degrees of freedom" in analysis problems? (**4**)

4. What method is widely used in medical research, library indexing, market research, criminal records and property records? What feature is common to these data? (**6**)

CHAPTER XXIV

Machine Analysis

1. Introduction. Analysis can be performed by using four types of machine:

(*a*) the cash register analysis type, which automatically provides a sales analysis, including VAT, as receipts are written;

(*b*) a key-operated accounting machine;

(*c*) punched card machines; and

(*d*) an electronic computer (dealt with in XXV).

2. Punched card accounting. While basically for multiple analysis, punched cards can be used for any normal accounting purposes, e.g. for preparation of sales invoices, monthly statements, etc.

(*a*) It makes use of manila cards of uniform size, each of which has pre-determined punching positions numbered 0–9 in vertical columns right across the card.

(*b*) The standard card has 80 columns, so that there is room for most standard information associated with a sales invoice—reference number, name of customer, quantity of goods, type of goods, price, extension, VAT, etc.

(*c*) Information is recorded by punching holes in the appropriate positions in the appropriate columns, according to the field of punching, i.e. heads of analysis.

3. Punched card system and basic machines. The stages in a basic punched card system consist of:

(*a*) coding;

(*b*) verifying;

(*c*) sorting; and

(*d*) tabulating.

4. Coding.

(*a*) Information put into the cards should preferably be in numerical form. It can be punched alphabetically, i.e. in alphanumeric form, but it is more economical of card if numerical.

(*b*) The first step, therefore, is to translate all the information to be analysed into numerical codes.

(*c*) To do this, a punching docket is often prepared with appropriate analysis headings on it.

5. Punching.

(*a*) After coding, the documents are passed to a punch operator, who records the information in the cards by means of a hand punch or an automatic key punch. Both machines have a simplified keyboard (*see* XXI, 2).

(*b*) When the appropriate key is pressed it punches a hole in a column in the card and the carriage holding the card moves along to the next column and so on.

(*c*) With the AKP (automatic key punch), the pattern of punching of the whole card is set up and is then punched electrically into the card at the completion of the setting up.

6. Sorting.

(*a*) When a number of cards representing a batch of (say) invoices has been punched and verified they are fed into a sorting machine, which is set to sort out a particular column on the cards. *It sorts out only one column at a time.*

(*b*) The sorting sequence is as follows:

(*i*) First sort according to the units, and collect cards from the pockets.

(*ii*) Replace cards in the hopper and press switch to sort according to the tens; collect.

(*iii*) Replace and sort according to the hundreds.

(*iv*) And so on.

(*c*) If sorting of numbered documents ever has to be done by hand, the sequence is the same as with the machine: by units, collect, tens, collect, hundreds, collect, and so on.

7. Tabulating.

(*a*) After sorting to the analysis required, the cards are fed to a tabulator which:

(*i*) senses the information punched in the cards (all or any of it);

(*ii*) prints it on sheets of paper (usually continuous stationery);

(*iii*) automatically adds up the various totals for the analyses required; and

(*iv*) prints the totals of them at the end of each section.

(*b*) The tabulator has a plugged programme control board by which instructions are given to the machine as to the information to be printed, which totals are to be printed, etc.

NOTE: The basic machines used are:
   (1) punch (hand punch or AKP);
   (2) verifier (direct verifier or automatic verifier);
   (3) sorter; and
   (4) tabulator.

8. Auxiliary machines. Large punched card installations invariably include various auxiliary machines, the main ones in use being:

(*a*) *Gang punch.* Automatically punches a pattern of holes in a number of cards at the same time (useful, for example, when putting the same date in a number of cards).

(*b*) *Reproducing punch.* Automatically punches duplicate sets of cards, on which the information being reproduced can be amended as desired.

(*c*) *Summary card punch.* Automatically punches a summary card in the course of tabulation. Thus, when analysing wages, it facilitates the gaining of cumulative totals of analysis headings for costing purposes.

(*d*) *Collator (or interpolator).* Automatically compares different sets of cards and punches, interfiles or segregates cards as desired. It can be used for verifying one set of cards with another identical set, and will automatically signal mistakes in the sequence of the cards.

(*e*) *Calculating punch.* Multiplies or divides quantities and amounts contained in the cards and punches the products into new cards (useful for invoice preparation). Figures punched in a card can be multiplied by a factor in the same card or by a group multiplier punched in a single "master" card.

(*f*) *Interpreter.* Prints the punched information on a card in ordinary language on the face of the card (alphabetical or numerical) or prints it on another plain card (transfer interpreter); it is an electronic device.

(*g*) *Mark senser.* An electronic machine which senses marking by graphite pencil in appropriate positions on the cards and automatically punches the information in the cards. This saves the need for punching documents and normal punching.

NOTE: One punched card system on the market claims that its tabulator is a combined tabulator, summary card punch, multiplying punch and interpolator.

9. Advantages of punched cards.

(*a*) Speed and economy of labour (mostly junior labour used).

(*b*) More control information for management and quicker than previously.

(*c*) Sorting, tabulating, etc., are all done automatically.

(*d*) With the addition of mark-sensing, the process becomes fully automatic.

(*e*) They facilitate multiple analysis of the same information.

10. Disadvantages of punched cards.

(*a*) Problems of integrating machine stages, when used for different office purposes.

(*b*) Lack of flexibility (size of card is a limiting factor).

(*c*) When estimating costs, it is difficult to forecast breakdown time, regulating and feeding time, etc.

(*d*) Difficulty which may be found in obtaining co-operation and confidence in the machines from all departments.

11. Uses of punched cards.

(*a*) Invoicing, using continuous stationery invoices and pre-punched sets of commodity cards and customer cards.

(*b*) Statistical tabulations and analysis.

(*c*) Sales analysis.

(*d*) Stock control.

(*e*) Wages preparation, with the pay-roll in continuous stationery form.

(*f*) Cheque preparation, with cheques in continuous stationery form.

(*g*) Record purposes, where the cards are retained as the records of the transactions.

(*h*) Analysis of wages for costing purposes.

NOTE: In many cases, several functions will be combined in one operation, e.g. sales analysis, costing, stock control, budgetary control, etc.

12. Factors to consider before adopting punched cards.

(*a*) Volume of work to be performed.

(*b*) The extent to which the transactions are of a uniform nature (if too diverse, punched card systems present many problems).

(*c*) Are multiple analyses required (the more they are, the more suitable is a punched card system)?

(*d*) Relative availability of accounting clerks and typists compared with unskilled punch operators.

(*e*) Savings in labour effected by use of the machines.

(*f*) Availability of maintenance.

(*g*) If they are to be used for invoicing, is the range of products fixed?

(*h*) Availability of sound-proof accommodation.

(*i*) Economy in cost compared with conventional accounting machines.

13. New technology. As described in previous chapters, (notably XXII, **12**) the dynamic advance of microtechnology and word-processing continues to render obsolete not only established office machines, but also entire office systems. The store (or memory) of the very wide range of devices available and the instantaneous retrieval of stored data provides, for example, all the output described under the uses of punched cards (*see* **11**).

Inevitably there will be a decline in the use of equipment mentioned in this chapter, but the student must continue to assume that its use will persist in smaller offices.

PROGRESS TEST 24

1. Describe how you would instruct a junior clerk to operate a sorting machine. (**5–7**)

2. Describe the functions of gang punch, verifier, sorter, tabulator and collator. (**7, 8**)

3. (*a*) What alternative is there to punching holes in cards, yet enjoying all the advantages of machine analysis? (*b*) How would you arrange to have for every punched card another card with corresponding words and figures? (**8**)

4. State the major advantages and disadvantages of a punched card system. (**9, 10**)

5. What factors must be considered before adopting punched cards? (**12**)

6. Assuming the use of 80 column cards, describe the type of information you would punch for a standard costing system.

CHAPTER XXV

Electronic Computers

1. Introduction. Electronics is that branch of electrical engineering which utilises transistors. Of the two main types of computer—digital and analog—the office is concerned only with the first, the second being used only for advanced technological purposes—aircraft simulation, etc.

Digital computers employ the scale of two (binary arithmetic), because a transistor has two phases only—off, representing zero, and on, representing one. Table VI compares the usual denary scale (ten) with the binary scale (two).

TABLE VI: Comparison of Denary and Binary Scale.

10^3	10^2	10^1	10^0	2^6	2^5	2^4	2^3	2^2	2^1	2^0
Denary scale				*Corresponding binary scale*						
			1							1
			2						1	0
			3						1	1
			4					1	0	0
			5					1	0	1
			6					1	1	0
			7					1	1	1
			8				1	0	0	0
			9				1	0	0	1
		1	0				1	0	1	0
1	2	7		1	1	1	1	1	1	1

The computer automatically converts the denary input to binary and prints the output in denary.

2. Definition. An electronic computer is an office machine by which office data is processed electronically at great speed (note the term "electronic data processing"): this means the performance of calculations, analyses, and printing the results. A computer is different from a mere calculator, in as much as it has a memory where many units of information (bits) can be stored until required.

A computer has five basic component parts:

(a) *Input*. It accepts information fed to it in the form of:
   (i) punched cards;
   (ii) punched tape; and sometimes
   (iii) magnetic tape.
Probably punched tape is the fastest input, and a common method is to reproduce the information in punched cards, which are then automatically converted to punched tape form.

(b) *Arithmetic unit*. That part of a computer which performs the calculations desired at remarkable speeds (e.g. 10,000 sums of two six-figure numbers in one second). Any calculation that can be done with figures can be done on a computer.

(c) *Control unit*, by which the sequence and the instructions are given to the machine as to what it has to do at each stage of its programmes.

(d) *Storage* (*or memory*) *unit*, where a series of figures can be stored, worked upon (e.g. increased by posting)—updated—and a new balance figure stored in place of the original one.

Various memory devices include:
   (i) nickel delay line (small capacity);
   (ii) magnetic core (quick random access);
   (iii) magnetic drum (quick random access, but more expensive);
   (iv) magnetic discs (quick random access);
   (v) magnetic tape (most economical method); and
   (vi) probably magnetic tape first, and magnetic discs next, are the most popular methods of providing the memory.
   (vii) Random-access floppy disc units. A floppy disc is a form of magnetic recording medium used in word-processing and data processing. It permits random access to stored data so that rapid search and retrieval is possible regardless of where the data are located on the disc.

(e) *Output*, where information is given back by the machine, again usually in the form of punched cards or punched tape, and where these can be fed to other machines for conversion into ordinary language. This is generally necessary because the vast speed of output is many times greater than that of the normal printing devices.

NOTE: A computer in the course of its operations and in accordance with its programme makes decisions by choosing between two alternatives—at lightning speed. Thus, in a pay-roll application, it will in connection with National Insurance deductions sense whether the employee is "under or over 18 years of age" (from data in the punched cards) and will accordingly route the process to the appropriate amount of deduction.

3. Installing a computer. Complete installations may take as long as two years, which time may be occupied by the following operations:

(*a*) Feasibility study to see if a computer is possible and advisable (this may take eight or nine months).

(*b*) Inquiry into the various computers available, and exploration with sales representatives of the application (up to six months).

(*c*) Systems analysis and writing of programmes (some programmes in themselves take over a year to write).

(*d*) Installation of the computer, possibly with its running in parallel with existing systems (computer programming must be thoroughly tested before it is adopted).

4. Systems analysis and programming. These are two separate steps.

(*a*) One consists of analysing all the processing of data through the business—a thorough-going O & M inquiry.

(*b*) The other consists of compiling a programme or sequence of steps in the working of a particular office system where calculations are involved.

(*c*) Office work usually requires a large number of small calculations in a chain sequence, and a great deal of work is involved in compiling suitable programmes.

5. Integrated data processing. This is the name (IDP for short) given to the method of application of a computer, such as when it is performing the data processing for one department (e.g. wages and calculations and preparation of pay-roll) and at the same time analyses the same data for another department (e.g. analyses for costing). Similarly, when processing sales invoices, it can provide figures for stock control and production control.

6. Advantages of a computer.

(*a*) Speed of operation, and the production of control information not previously available to management.

(b) Greater accuracy of the figures provided.

(c) Savings effected by better management control (e.g. quick return of periodic stock figures).

(d) Once information is in computer language, all processing of it is automatic.

(e) Savings in labour because of (d).

(f) Flexibility: it can be used for many purposes in a business.

7. Disadvantages of a computer.

(a) It entails upheaval and change of all existing office systems (usually easier if punched cards are already used).

(b) It often means two years of preparatory work before any results are seen from its application.

(c) Difficulty of obtaining experienced systems analysts and programmers.

(d) Capital outlay (although many are rented today).

(e) Breakdown and maintenance troubles (particularly serious when the computer is processing *all* the data for all departments).

(f) There are continual advances in the development of computers, and by the time it is installed it may be out of date.

8. Uses of a computer.
A computer can be used for any office job which involves figures, but the following applications are most popular:

(a) *Pay-roll work:*
   (i) it produces the pay-roll;
   (ii) calculates tax liability; and
   (iii) produces statements of pay and cash analysis.

(b) *Costing and budgetary control* from figures of labour and material posted from the pay-roll and stores procedures.
   (i) Comparisons can be made automatically with the budgeted figures; and
   (ii) the machine discovers variances, when significant differences are brought to light.

(c) *Stock control:*
   (i) The machine automatically compares levels of different stocks with pre-set minima and reveals when re-ordering is required.
   (ii) Lists of stock items can be obtained any time.
   (iii) Postings can be made to stock accounts in the same way as to ledger accounts.

(d) *Sales accounting:*

(i) Pricing and discount data can be held in the storage unit, to be called on when required.

(ii) Various departmental copies can be prepared at the same time as sales invoices.

(iii) Credit control is obtained at the same time, because the machine will compare each invoice with the credit limit of each customer.

(iv) Statement production and ledger posting can be done at the same time as sales invoicing.

(e) *Production planning:*

(i) Material scheduling and plant loading are calculated automatically.

(ii) An important use of the digital computer in the context of production planning is that of linear programming, of which the following problem is a simple example.

EXAMPLE:
A manufacturer of energy fuel has a schedule of weight, energy and cost per unit of three alternative substances, as indicated in Table VII. One or more of the substances is to be used for the final output.

TABLE VII: A Linear Programming Problem.

Fuel type	A	B	C
Weight per unit volume (tonnes)	15	10	20
Energy per unit volume (units)	30	25	45
Cost per unit volume (£)	1	0.8	1.4

A mixture of 10 units of volume is to be made. The mixture must not exceed 160 tonnes in weight, must produce not less than 320 units of energy, and must be produced at minimum cost.

The computer technique for the solution of the above is:

(a) draft the programme;

(b) feed the programme (by any of the media defined in 2 (a)) into the store;

(c) put in the data of the problem;

(d) receive the print-out of the answer, which is shown in Table VIII.

TABLE VIII: Solution to Linear Programming Problem.

Fuel No.	Volume units	Tonnes	Energy	Minimum cost
B	6.5	65	162.5	5.2
C	3.5	70	157.5	4.9
Total	10.0	135	320.0	£10.1

(e) *Production planning:*

(i) Material scheduling and plant loading are calculated automatically.

(f) *Market research:*

(i) Analysis is made of all data collected.

(ii) Speed is often an important factor of this work.

(g) *Stock and share registration*, for which computers are widely used.

(i) The on-line alphabetical retrieval computer system with its memory bank is capable of registering share transfers in seconds and of retaining the details of what it has done.

(ii) Many modern companies entrust the whole of their share registration work, including the annual return, to specialists offering computer services.

(h) *Word-processing* is a comparative newcomer to the great range of computing.

(i) This is the automatic or semi-automatic manipulation of text electronically, and the automatic production of first-time final copy.

(ii) It is a way of ensuring that both one-off typescript, and standard script which is to be used more than once, is typed once and once only.

(iii) It is then stored on magnetic files for subsequent amendment and printing.

(iv) Its objective is to minimise duplication of work.

(v) An inherent factor in the installation of the system is the break-up of the traditional executive/secretary relationship.

9. Computer developments. In recent years, developments have been most prominent in:

(a) Smaller computers at low cost. The pocket programmables now on the market at prices under £20 are capable, combined with their extensive libraries of standard programmes, of handling many of the simpler types of linear programming of which an example was given in **8**.

(*b*) Larger computers with greater capacity.

(*c*) Random access devices (e.g. card random access, using magnetic cards) to give speed of recovery of individual items of data from a series recorded.

(*d*) Ability to send data automatically from a distant point over a telegraph or telephone wire which is automatically fed to the input of a computer.

(*e*) Direct input by the medium of "optical scanning" of magnetic ink characters (as used on cheques by banks).

(*f*) The use of VDUs (visual display units) also for direct input.

(*g*) The use of computer bureaux, instead of buying a computer.

10. Factors to consider when purchasing a computer.

(*a*) Suitability to the business (the advantages should be compared with the disadvantages).

(*b*) Capital outlay, although this is likely to be spread over a number of years.

(*c*) Form of input and output.

(*d*) Speed of input and output.

(*e*) What kind of memory and what capacity (usually measured in K, i.e. 1000 bits) would be most suitable?

(*f*) Speed of random access.

(*g*) Whether to have IDP straight away or to put one department only on a computer basis (it is usually advisable to work up to IDP).

(*h*) Whether suitable staff are available or, if not, what training is required and how to provide it.

11. The National Data Processing Service (NDPS). This is the commercial arm of Post Office computing, which offers commerce and industry a wide range of computer bureaux services. These include:

(*a*) processing capacity on powerful computers;

(*b*) systems design and programming;

(*c*) computer to microfilm facilities;

(*d*) file conversion and data preparation;

(*e*) programme development aids and training;

(*f*) IRIS (inventory recording and invoicing system).

12. Database management system (DBMS). A database and its control mechanism, the database management system, together represent a highly sophisticated computerised method of storing, organising and retrieving information, using magnetic storage media.

(a) The objectives are to maximise the efficiency of use of the computer itself.

(b) *Database* refers to the collection of stored information.

(c) *Database management system* refers to the control software package which is responsible for organising and accessing the information.

13. The "micro revolution". A microcomputer makes use of the almost magic capacity of the silicon chip to store and process information at a very low cost. Miniaturisation of circuits has led to a dramatic reduction in computing costs. It is estimated that the cost of computing power has been falling at an annual rate of about 40 per cent for ten years or more. To-day's microcomputer is as powerful as the bulky main-frame computers of 25 years ago.

The essential difference between the microcomputer and its older brothers is that it is a powerful tool of management: it sits on the manager's desk. By using its simple keyboard he can ask the questions: e.g. What was yesterday's total turnover? How much cash was banked? What is the current balance? What is the debtors' position? Is a particular item in stock? The answers appear on the screen in front of him.

As described in previous chapters, microprocessing and word-processing have revolutionised office systems and imparted a most powerful impetus to thrusting, creative management.

PROGRESS TEST 25

1. What are the two most impressive aspects of an electronic computer? **(2, 6)**

2. What is the importance of a feasibility study? **(3)**

3. Distinguish between systems analysis and programming. **(4)**

4. What are the major disadvantages of a computer? **(7)**

5. Examine the importance of computers in the context of budgetary control. **(8)**

6. What are the major arguments against the use of a computer bureau to handle the share registration work of a large company? **(8)**

7. Draft a simple linear programming problem from your own experience. **(8)**

8. Outline the major recent developments in computering.   **(9)**

9. What is the NPDS? **(11)**

10. What is random access?

11. Briefly assess the significance of the "micro-revolution". **(13)**

PART THREE

RECORDS AND GENERAL SERVICES

CHAPTER XXVI

Sales Invoicing, Purchasing and Stock Control

1. Importance of efficient sales invoicing.

(*a*) Prompt rendering of the invoice promotes quick receipt of cash.

(*b*) An efficient system minimises risk of fraud in a sensitive area of the company's assets.

2. Speed in invoicing. Speed in sales invoicing can be obtained by using the following machines and equipment.

(*a*) Invoices in continuous stationery form.
(*b*) Punched card machines.
(*c*) Addressing machines.
(*d*) Photocopying machines.
(*e*) Computers.
(*f*) Accounting machines.
(*g*) Spirit duplicating machines.

3. Fraud prevention. Some of the steps than can be taken:

(*a*) Ensure that sales invoices are pre-numbered, and that a check is made on serial numbering when posting to ledger accounts.

(*b*) Produce invoice, advice note, instruction to transport and warehouse or factory simultaneously.

(*c*) Ensure that goods are sent out only on receipt of official orders.

(*d*) use internal check systems and internal audit.

4. Choice of invoicing machinery. This will depend, among other things, on:

(*a*) the volume of sales;
(*b*) the number of copies of invoices required;
(*c*) the variation in the number of copies for different customers;

(d) the availability of skilled typists;

(e) the analysis required.

5. Credit control. In practice a credit limit is defined for each customer. The limit is normally marked on the ledger card, but, following experience of the individual customers, the limit may be exceeded at the discretion of, and with the express authority of, the credit controller, since too rigid an application of control may hinder an expansion of turnover. The major purpose of control is to minimise bad debts.

With a new customer, inquiries are made of:

(a) his bank, using the good offices of the company's own bank;

(b) business associates and customers, i.e. trade references;

(c) status inquiry agents;

(d) trade associations.

6. Purchase invoices. The basis of an efficient system is as follows:

(a) Copies of all orders placed by the buying department are sent to the accounts department. Similar copies (without prices) are sent to the goods inwards department.

(b) As goods are received they are entered by the goods inwards department on goods received sheets, numbered consecutively. The goods inwards clerk cross references the sheets (or goods inward book folio) with the bin cards or other stock records. Checking the stores records is one of the basic routines of internal audit.

(c) When the purchases invoices arrive they are at once stamped:

(i) with the time and date of receipt;

(ii) with a rubber stamp in the basic form shown in Fig. 5.

(d) The supervisor passes the invoices for payment by initialling them.

Order No.		Initials
Goods inwards ref.		
Quantities checked		
Prices & VAT checked		
Extensions checked		
Passed for payment		

FIG. 5   *Rubber stamp for purchase invoices.*

(*e*) Any invoices qualifying for cash discount if paid within, say, seven days, receive priority treatment by being sent to the cashier for immediate payment. Invoices not so qualifying are attached to the relevant monthly statements submitted by the suppliers and passed to the cashier for payment at the end of the month.

7. Stock control. Few clerical activities are more important than efficient control of stock, the basic elements of which include the following.

(*a*) Ensure an efficient buying department—the buyers should be properly qualified, e.g. by membership of the Institute of Purchasing and Supply, together with relevant practical experience.

(*b*) Regular recording of receipt of goods. Do not leave this job to juniors, ensure responsible supervision.

(*c*) Issue goods from stock only on submission of an official requisition or release-note signed by a responsible person.

(*d*) Keep adequate stock records always up-to-date.

(*e*) Take stock regularly and properly.

8. Stocktaking. There are two main methods.

(*a*) *Perpetual inventory.*

(*i*) A section of the stock is checked at regular intervals, thereby checking the entire stock throughout the year.

(*ii*) Discrepancies discovered are at once reported to the management.

(*iii*) At the end of the year the stock-book figures are taken as the physical closing stock, without further stocktaking.

(*b*) *Yearly stocktaking*, by which all stock on hand at the end of the financial year are counted, classified and valued.

9. Principles of stocktaking.

(*a*) Fix commencing and finishing dates and draw up a time-table.

(*b*) Settle responsibility for supervision and consider the effect on flexible working hours.

(*c*) Decide the date after which purchases are not to be included. Only materials recorded in the purchases journal should be included in the stock-taking.

(*d*) Decide on the method of stocktaking. Is the time taken commensurate with the degree of accuracy required?

(*e*) Decide on the method of valuation of stock, e.g. FIFO, LIFO, average value, etc.

10. Value added tax (VAT).

(a) At each stage of business activity a taxable person is charged with VAT on the goods and services supplied to him by his suppliers.

(b) Those goods and services are called his *inputs*, and the tax on them, which appears on the purchase invoice rendered by the supplier, is his *input tax*.

(c) When he in turn supplies goods and services, not necessarily the same ones, to his customers, he charges them with VAT: the goods and services are *outputs* and the tax which he charges (appearing on his sales invoices) is his *output tax*.

(d) At intervals, when he has to make a return to the Customs and Excise, he totals all output tax and all input tax and deducts the smaller from the greater; the difference is the amount he has to pay to Customs and Excise or which will be repaid to him.

EXAMPLE:

	Purchases invoices	*Sales invoices*
Goods and services	£3000	£4600
Add VAT (15 per cent)*	£450	£690

At the end of the period (normally three months) he has to pay £690 less £450 = £240 to Customs and Excise.
* Rate in August 1981

(e) VAT necessarily complicates the drafting of sales invoices and the checking of purchases invoices, and its administration is an added strain both for the training of staff and the operation of departments concerned with invoices, and the payment, or reclaiming, of VAT.

(f) The invoicing system can be integrated with the sales ledger for immediate posting of invoice and credit note totals to a sales accounting module.

Instant retrieval of stock information and therefore control of stock by "spot-check" is facilitated by the use of microcomputers which are rapidly becoming smaller and simpler. Their use enables a manager to key into his business from almost anywhere, to ascertain stock levels, to distribute memoranda to his colleagues, instruct his secretary, etc. before he leaves for the office. Prestel (*see* XXXI) greatly extends the range of the modern manager in obtaining up-to-the-minute information about prices, etc. enabling him to buy, or withhold, goods for the purpose of economic stockholding of his own company.

11. New techniques in invoicing and stock control. The "micro revolution" described in XXV has a far-reaching effect on many of the traditional methods described in this chapter. A typical modern invoicing unit has the following main characteristics:

(*a*) Parameters, set up to the individual user's own requirements, control all aspects of the invoice design, style and layout: heading information, content of invoice columns, order of printing columns, VAT calculation and printing, discounts by customer, product and quantity. Any of these design controls can be readily altered without costly programming.

(*b*) All customer details are maintained on file, including special discount rates, VAT indicators etc. When an account number is keyed at the start of an invoice, the name and address is drawn from file and displayed on the computer's video screen. Optional facilities in this extremely flexible system include automatic printing of branch names, subtitles, messages and terms of trade.

PROGRESS TEST 26

1. Why is speed in invoicing imperative? What devices may be used to attain speed? **(1, 2)**

2. What effect might: (*a*) slack credit control; (*b*) rigid credit control; have on a business? **(5)**

3. Summarise the basic control over processing purchase invoices. **(6)**

4. What procedure relating to stock control would you insist upon being rigorously observed? **(7)**

5. A purchase invoice for a large amount has been entered on 31st December (the last day of the company's financial year) in the Purchases Journal although the goods have not yet been taken into stock. On what grounds would you include them in the annual stocktaking, assuming that they arrived on the following day? **(9)**

6. What is VAT, and what additional responsibilities does it impose on office administration? **(10)**

7. What effect will new techniques have on conventional methods of (*a*) invoicing; (*b*) stock control? **(11)**

CHAPTER XXVII

Wages Systems

1. Methods of payment.

(*a*) In cash (usually weekly wages).

(*b*) By cheque (usually monthly salaries).

(*c*) By traders' credit (usually monthly salaries).

2. Wages system. It is usual to give every worker a pay number or clock number, both as a means of identification and as a check against fraud. The subsequent steps in a wages system will usually include the following:

(*a*) Checking on attendance and work records, according to whether wages are paid on a time or piecework basis.

(*b*) Calculation of gross pay. This will often comprise:

(*i*) flat rate earnings;

(*ii*) overtime earnings;

(*iii*) production bonus;

(*iv*) time-keeping bonus, etc.

(*c*) Entry of deductions from gross pay (some are compulsory, such as National Insurance and PAYE tax, and some voluntary).

(*d*) Calculation of net pay.

(*e*) Preparation of statements of pay.

(*f*) Enter employer's and employee's National Insurance contributions and income tax on the official deduction card, P11, for each employee.

(*g*) Cash analysis, and drawing cash from the bank (or drafting of cheques or traders' credit slips).

(*h*) "Bagging up" the cash, i.e. placing it in pay envelopes.

(*i*) Distribution of envelopes to employees.

(*j*) Within 14 days of the end of every month remit to the Inland Revenue the PAYE (net of refunds) and the employer's NI contributions.

3. Machines and equipment. Almost every kind of office machine is used in connection with wages, depending on the size of the business and the complexity of the wages calculations.

(*a*) Accounting machine (or writing board) on which the pay-roll, tax-deduction record and statement of pay can be produced simultaneously.

(*b*) Addressing machines for the prior preparation of the pay-roll and for inserting the pay numbers and names on pay envelopes.

(*c*) Calculating machine, for calculation of gross pay.

(*d*) Adding machine, for adding columns on the pay-roll.

(*e*) Coin-issuing and note-counting machines, when bagging-up.

(*f*) Punched card machines, with the pay-roll in continuous stationery form.

(*g*) A computer for larger pay-rolls.

4. Prevention of "dummy" wages. This means preventing a dishonest employee from entering fictitious names on the pay-roll and then paying the cash to himself.

(*a*) Divide the duties among different members of the staff (or different departments in a large business), e.g. for the calculation, drawing cash from the bank, paying-out, etc. This will at least deter collusion among staff.

(*b*) Include the occasional checking of the pay-roll against personnel records among the routines of internal audit.

(*c*) Institute a system of identification before paying wages (some business concerns use the time card for this purpose).

(*d*) Pay wages as well as salaries by cheque or traders' credit (*see* **6**).

(*e*) Always ensure that unclaimed wages, e.g. due to illness of the employee, are properly explained, and that unclaimed pay packets are returned to the safe, pending the personal appearance of those entitled to them.

(*f*) Periodically reconcile the pay numbers issued by the personnel department with those on the pay-roll and on the clock cards or other time-keeping records.

5. Prevention of theft. Apart from the obvious precautions of keeping cash in the office safe and locking the office (and windows) during lunch-time, the most likely theft is by "payroll bandits" on the way from the bank. Steps that can be taken include:

(*a*) Varying the routes taken to and from the bank (busy streets are safer).

(*b*) Providing suitable escorts (not old age pensioners).

(*c*) Planning the route in detail, so that there is no hesitation at the kerbside.

(*d*) Drawing cash from the bank during normal banking hours.

(*e*) Carrying banknotes on the person.

(*f*) Using special security bags or boxes for holding cash.

(*g*) Using a suitable vehicle, if possible a different one each time.

(*h*) Checking the characters of all employees involved.

(*i*) When exceptionally large amounts are involved, informing the police beforehand.

(*j*) Verify that relevant insurance policies are adequate, and being maintained.

(*k*) Engage the services of Securicor or another cash-carrying agency.

6. Payment of Wages Act 1960. This Act was instituted to avoid the difficulties presented by the Truck Acts, which state that wages must be paid "in coin of the Realm", as some employers wanted legal powers to pay wages by cheque.

(*a*) It legalises the payment of wages to an employee:

(*i*) By cheque or by traders' credit, if the employee requests it in writing and the employer does not refuse. Many employers act on employees' mandate to credit their accounts at named branches of a bank with the amount of the wage or salary.

(*ii*) By postal order (without request) when employees are absent through sickness or injury.

(*b*) The employer is not allowed to make any deduction for payment in any of the specified ways.

(*c*) Where any of such method of payment is used, the employee must be given, at or before the time of payment, a detailed statement of pay.

(*d*) Either party may cancel the arrangement at any time by giving four weeks' notice or both parties can agree in writing to end it immediately.

7. Payment of wages by cheque.

(*a*) *Advantages*.

(*i*) Cheques can be prepared more quickly and economically than payment in cash.

(*ii*) It overcomes to some extent the risk of theft in transit.

(*iii*) Employees with large pay packets are encouraged to open bank accounts and have cheque facilities.

(*iv*) It is a safer method of payment from the employer's point of view.

(*b*) *Disadvantages*.

(*i*) Workers generally prefer to receive cash.

(*ii*) It transfers the risk to the bank.

(*iii*) Employees do not always want bank accounts.

(*iv*) Bank hours are inconvenient to employees.

8. Statutory deductions from gross pay: PAYE and NI. Important changes in the recording of Pay, Tax and National Insurance contributions, and End of Year returns came into effect from 6 April 1981. The Pay As You Earn method of deducting income tax from salaries and wages applies to *all* income from offices or employments (except those held by certain divers and their supervisors) and in a few isolated employments for which special provisions exist. Thus, PAYE applies to the following:

(*a*) weekly wages;

(*b*) monthly salaries;

(*c*) annual salaries;

(*d*) bonuses;

(*e*) commissions;

(*f*) directors' fees;

(*g*) any other income from an office or employment.

The term "employee" for PAYE purposes includes office holders (e.g. directors) and pensioners.

TABLE IX: PAYE and National Insurance "thresholds".

Deductions must be made for all employees whose rate of pay exceeds the following "thresholds":

Date from which applied	Code for emergency use	PAYE threshold		NI contributions: lower earnings limit	
		weekly	monthly	weekly	monthly
(1)	(2)	(3)	(4)	(5)	(6)
6/4/1983	156L	£30.00	£131.00	£32.50	£140.83

The above figures may be updated later.

9. The employer has the choice of any of the following four ways.

(*a*) He may use the official Working Sheet (form P11 (New)) for recording the figures on each pay day and enter the totals on the official End of Year Return (Form P14) *See* **11** for a facsimile of form P11 (New).

(*b*) He may incorporate the figures in his own pay records each pay day and enter the totals on the official End of Year Return (P14).

(*c*) He may incorporate the figures in his own pay records each pay day and use a proprietary or own-design end of year document in substitution for P14.

Deductions working sheet P11 (New)

Employer's name ....

Employee's surname (in BLOCK letters) ....

Employee's first two forenames ....

Tax District and reference ....

National Insurance no. ....

Works no. etc. ....

Year to 5 April 19 ......

Tax Code†	Amended code†	Week (Month) no. in which applied

National Insurance Contributions*

Total of Employee's & of Employer's Contributions 1a	Employee's Contributions payable 1b	Employee's contributions at Contracted-out rate included in column 1c

MONTH / WEEK number

Pay in the week or month 2	Total pay to date 3	Total free pay to date as shown by Table A 4	Total taxable pay to date 5	Total tax due to date as shown by Taxable Pay Tables 6	Tax deducted or refunded in the week or month (mark refunds "R") 7	For employer's use

PAYE Income Tax

Date of birth in figures — Day, Month, Year

Date of leaving in figures — Day, Month, Year

MONTH / WEEK rows:
April to May 5 (1, 2, 3, 4)
May to June 5 (5, 6, 7, 8)
June to July 5 (9, 10, 11, 12, 13)
July to Aug 5 (14, 15, 16, 17)
Aug to Sept 5 (18, 19, 20, 21)
Sept to Oct 5 (22, 23, 24, 25, 26)
Oct to Nov 5 (27, 28, 29, 30)

Total carried forward | Total carried forward | Total carried forward

*N.I. Contribution Table letter must be entered overleaf beside the N.I. totals boxes – see the note shown there. This box may be used if the employer wishes to record the N.I. letter while this side of the sheet is in use.

† If amended cross out previous code.

* If in any week/month the amount in column 4 is more than the amount in column 3, make no entry in column 5.

P11 (New)

FIG. 6 Form P11 (New)—front.

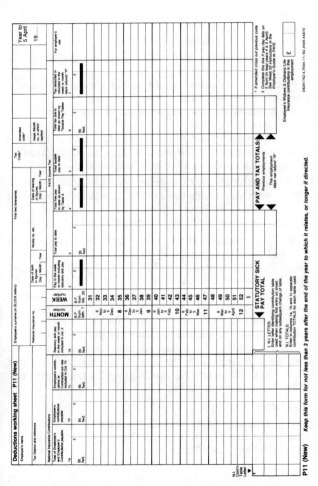

FIG. 6 *Form P11 (New)—back.*

(*d*) He may incorporate the figures in his own computerised pay records and make an end of year return for each employee on magnetic tape.

10. Facsimile of form P11 (New) (see Fig. 6). This Deductions Working Sheet which the local tax office issues to employers is a good example of efficient form design:

(*a*) it is comprehensive in accommodating two distinct sets of statutory deductions.

(*b*) it is flexible in providing for employees paid at weekly, monthly or at other intervals.

(*c*) it is economical, both sides of the card being used.

(*d*) it is durable.

(*e*) it does not differ fundamentally from the previous P11 (old) form; in combination with the instructions on the Blue Card (P8) it is relatively straightforward to understand and use.

The Working Sheets once completed must be kept intact for at least *three* years after the end of the year to which they relate, or longer if the Inland Revenue requires. They are *not* to be sent to the Collector of Taxes at the end of the year.

11. End of year returns (P14). Unless the employer chooses method (*c*) or (*d*) of **9**, he must complete, for each employee, the three-part form P14. One impression suffices if a ball-point pen is used.

Parts one and two are sent to the Collector of Taxes in *two* separate bundles for onward transmission to the Department of Health and Social Security and the Tax Office respectively.

The third part of P14 is the P60 certificate to be given to the employee so long as he is in the employer's employment at 5 April. The basic entries on P14 are total pay and total tax due for the year (or from 6 April until the date of leaving), the totals of employer's and employee's NI contributions, together with personal details, code numbers, etc.

12. Tax tables. These are:

Book 1. Free pay tables (Tables A) showing for each code (notified to the employer by the Tax Office and entered on P11 (New)) the free pay (not affected by tax) for each income tax week or year.

Book 2. Taxable Pay Tables (Tables B to D). These show tax due on taxable pay to date (i.e. pay to date less free pay to date as shown in the A tables of Book 1).

Book 3. Tax reckoner for prefix F codes (for higher rates of tax).

13. Form 45. When an employee leaves, parts 2 & 3 of form 45 must be handed to him or her. Part 1 of the form must be sent immediately to the tax office.

14. New employee. When a new employee is engaged, he or she should at once be asked for parts 2 and 3 of form P45, which was issued by the previous employer. The new employer sends Part 3 to the Tax Office and prepares a Deductions Working Sheet (P11 New) in accordance with instructions on Part 2 and the Blue Card (P8).

15. Payment of tax to the collector. The total of tax deducted, less any tax refunded, during an income tax month must be paid to the Collector within *fourteen days* of the end of that month. It is sufficient to send a single remittance to cover this tax payment and any National Insurance contributions that may be due. A payslip (P30B(Z) or P30(Z)) should be sent with each payment showing the division of the total into PAYE and NI.

16. NI contributions. From the tax year beginning 6 April 1981 NI contributions will be recorded, together with PAYE deductions on form P11 (new)—the Deductions Working Sheet. An employer using substitute end-of-year documents or submitting end-of-year returns in magnetic tape form, however, is not affected by changes in the official deduction cards. Under the Social Security Pensions Act 1975, pensions for retirement, widowhood and invalidity become earnings-related instead of flat-rate. A new pension consists of:

(*a*) a basic, flat-rate pension, and

(*b*) an additional pension, related to an employee's reckonable earnings above those necessary for the basic pension.

Employees who are members of occupational pension schemes which meet specific requirements can be contracted out, by their employers, of the additional part of retirement pension and the additional part of widow's pension. Contracted-out employees and their employers will pay the normal rate of contribution on earnings up to and including the lower earnings limit, plus a lower rate of contribution on earnings between the lower and upper earnings limits.

The limits are defined in Table X below. It is an extract from the leaflet NI 40 issued by the Department of Health and Social Security.

TABLE X: Class 1 Contributions for Employees and Employers
(*see Leaflet NI 40*)

Lower earnings limit	Upper earnings limit
£29.50 a week	£220.00 a week
£127.85 a month	£953.33 a month
£1,533.96 a year	£11,439.96 a year

Not contracted-out rates	Employee	Employer (*NI surcharge is included*)
Standard rate	8.75%	12.2%
Reduced rate for married women and widows with valid certificates of election (*reduced liability*)	3.20%	12.2%
Men over 65 and women over 60	Nil	12.2%
Children under 16	Nil	Nil
People earning under £29.50 a week*	Nil	Nil

Contracted-out rates	On first £29.50 a week	On earnings between £29.50 and £220.00 a week	On first £29.50 a week	On earnings between £29.50 and £220.00 a week
Standard rate	8.75%	6.25%	12.2%	7.7%
Reduced rate for married women and widows with valid certificates of election (*reduced liability*)	3.20%	3.20%	12.2%	7.7%
People earning under £29.50 a week*	Nil	—	Nil	—

* or monthly or other equivalent

17. New techniques. The rapid advance of microtechnology provides a range of payroll servicing methods which render obsolete much of the equipment described in **3**, although its use will continue in the non-automated office.

PROGRESS TEST 27

1. What is the practical importance of giving each employee a pay number? (**2**)

2. What machines and equipment can be used, and for what purposes, in the preparation and payment of wages? (**3**)

3. State the major methods of preventing fraud in a wages system. (**4**)

4. Examine the arguments in favour of paying wages other than by cash. (**6**)

5. What are the provisions of the Payment of Wages Act 1960? (**6**)

6. State the employer's four choices for recording and returning pay, tax and National Insurance contributions (**10**)

7. What do you understand by PAYE and NI "thresholds"? (**8**)

8. Describe the employer's duty in relation to PAYE and NI records at the end of the tax year (**12**)

9. State briefly how you would determine an employee's liability to tax in a given week. (**13**).

10. Define "contracted out employee" (**17**)

11. When must payment of PAYE and NI deductions be made, and to whom? (**16**)

12. Draft a simple "flow-diagram" to show the movements of the three parts of Form 45, which is required when an employee leaves (**14 & 15**)

CHAPTER XXVIII

Records and Filing

1. Introduction. Filing is the basis of record keeping; it entails the process of arranging and storing records so that they can be located when required.

2. Essentials of a good filing system. The word "system", in this connection, usually refers to the method of arrangement or classification, but it can also refer to the type of equipment used, to the organisation of staffing and to the methods used when referring to or borrowing records.

(*a*) *Compactness*. It should not take up too much space, particularly floor space.

(*b*) *Accessibility*. Record cabinets should be so sited that it is easy to file records or extract them.

(*c*) *Simplicity*. The system (particularly of classification) should be simple to understand and simple to operate.

(*d*) Safety. The right degree of safety should be given to the documents according to their relative importance.

(*e*) *Economy*. The system should be economical in money cost and in labour and overhead costs.

(*f*) *Elasticity*. The system should be capable of expansion when required.

(*g*) *Records* should be capable of being produced with the minimum delay possible.

(*h*) *Efficiency*. Cross-references should be provided where necessary, so that a document can be found under different headings.

(*i*) *Up-to-date*. Records should always be filed up-to-date, although this may depend on the staffing and on control.

(*j*) *Removal.* Some system of using "'out' guides" or "tracers" should indicate which documents have been removed, when and by whom.

(*k*) *Suitability*. The most appropriate system of classification should be used.

NOTE: There is no *best* system of filing; every office should have its filing systems tailor-made to suit its purposes.

3. Methods of filing. There are only two basic methods of filing records:

(*a*) *Flat filing*, where documents are placed on top of one another in drawers, etc. (perhaps entailing difficulty in finding paper required);

(*b*) *Vertical filing*, where documents are filed on edge, one behind the other, in the order of the classification adopted. Vertical filing is in almost universal use today, although flat files still have their uses for particular purposes, e.g. the keeping of current invoices (pending payment) in alphabetical order in a cabinet of shallow wooden trays, each indexed on the front with the appropriate letter.

4. Alphabetical classification. This is where documents are filed according to the first letters in the name and then in order of second names.

(*a*) A variation is *Vowel filing* where, in a small filing system documents are filed according to the first vowel in the name, e.g. BRIGHT would be filed under BI, etc.

(*b*) *Advantages.*

(*i*) Convenience of grouping papers by name of company, etc.

(*ii*) Direct filing, with no index.

(*iii*) Simple and easy to understand.

(*iv*) Useful provision for miscellaneous papers.

(*c*) *Disadvantages.*

(*i*) In large systems, it takes longer to find papers.

(*ii*) Congestion under common names.

(*iii*) Papers may reasonably be filed under different headings.

(*iv*) Difficulty of forecasting space requirements for different letters of the alphabet, although there is a standard frequency of distribution of UK business names and their initial letters.

(*d*) *Examples:* correspondence filing, contracts, staff records, etc.

NOTE: The Companies Act 1948, s. 111 (*i*), states that "every company having more than fifty members shall, unless the register of members is in such a form (e.g. alphabetical) as to constitute in itself an index, keep an index of the members of the company", and s. 111 (*ii*) continues that "the index shall contain a sufficient indication to enable the account in the register of members to be readily found".

5. Numerical classification. This is where each document or folder is given a number and filed in serial number order.

(*a*) A variation is the *terminal digit* system where filing is in the order of the terminal digits (this makes it easy to clear out dead material: no expansion problems).

(*b*) Another common variation is *decimal-numeric* (as used in libraries) where each class has 10 sub-divisions, each of which has 10 more sub-divisions, and so on.

(*c*) *Advantages.*

(*i*) Greater accuracy in filing.

(*ii*) The file number can be used as a reference.

(*iii*) Unlimited expansion is possible.

(*iv*) The index is a complete list and can be used for other purposes, e.g. as an address index.

(*d*) Disadvantages.

(*i*) More time required in referring to the index.

(*ii*) Files for miscellaneous papers are not so easy to arrange.

(*iii*) Cost of the index and space taken by it.

(*iv*) Transposition of figures causes errors in filing.

(*e*) *Examples:* filing of sales invoices, contracts (if numbered), orders, committee minutes, etc.

Thus a main subject group covering Insurance might be numbered 1.0 and the various types of insurance numbered 1.1, 1.2, 1.3, etc. respectively for Fire, Motor, Employers' Liability, etc. The decimal system is recommended when it is necessary to revise an existing system which has become an inefficient, time-consuming jumble.

6. Geographical classification. This is where the papers or files are divided according to geographical location. Either part, or full, geographical classification can be used, e.g. London, Provincial, and Overseas, for correspondence.

(*a*) *Advantages.*

(*i*) Convenience of reference where the location is known.

(*ii*) A measure of direct filing is usual.

(*b*) *Disadvantages.*

(*i*) Possibility of error where knowledge of geography is weak.

(*ii*) Geographical location must be known.

(*iii*) There may be a need for an occasional index.

(*c*) *Examples:* customers' orders in sales area order, filing of correspondence according to town, etc.

7. Subject classification. This is where the documents are arranged in accordance with the subject-matter, instead of with the names of the companies, correspondents, etc.

(*a*) Advantages
    (*i*) Convenience of reference when the subject alone is known.
    (*ii*) Unlimited expansion.
(*b*) *Disadvantages.*
    (*i*) Difficulty of classification.
    (*ii*) Not very suitable for miscellaneous papers.
    (*iii*) Liberal cross-references may be needed.
    (*iv*) An index may be needed.
(*c*) *Examples:* filing of orders according to materials in the buying department, filing of contracts, correspondence: legal, staff, etc.

8. Chronological classification. This is where the documents are filed in order of their date. This system is rarely used absolutely but it is the usual method of filing papers inside each folder.

(*a*) *Advantage.* Useful if dates are known.
(*b*) *Disadvantages.*
    (*i*) It is not always suitable.
    (*ii*) Incoming letters might become separated from outgoing ones.
(*c*) *Examples:* useful for a "tickler" file of letters which have answers outstanding.

9. Combinations of systems. Use can be made of combinations of systems (**4**) to (**8**), such as alphanumerical (B1, B2, B3, etc.), or correspondence classified as A for Food, B for Ice cream, C for Bread, etc. (alphabetically coded subject) or 1.1: Furniture (chairs), 1.2: Furniture (tables), etc. (numerically coded subject).

This is often the most flexible method, since the advantages of several classifications together may be obtained.

10. Factors in choosing classification.

(*a*) What is the most convenient method of reference?
(*b*) Size of the system (larger systems are usually numerical).
(*c*) Simplicity in use (the alphabetical system is usually simplest to understand).
(*d*) Ease of expansion (the numerical is easiest to expand).
(*e*) Does it minimise the possibility of misfiling?
(*f*) Does it give the greatest speed of location?

11. Central filing. This is where all (or some) of the records of a business are filed in one room together instead of in separate offices. It means that all papers about the same subjects from different departments are filed together on common files in the central filing department. Departments wishing to refer to papers then borrow the files from the central filing department.

Note that it is not always necessary to make a straight choice between central filing or departmental filing; in many business concerns an intermediate policy is followed whereby active or current papers are filed in the departments, while the central filing department is kept for reserve filing only.

(*a*) A central filing department would not be suitable:

(*i*) Where the business is geographically spread;

(*ii*) for confidential documents (e.g. personnel records); or

(*iii*) for documents which are the concern of one department only.

(*b*) *Advantages.*

(*i*) Uniformity of filing procedures.

(*ii*) Development of specialist filing staff.

(*iii*) Improved supervision of filing and records.

(*iv*) It fixes the responsibility for filing (which is often done by anyone inside a department).

(*v*) It ensures that all correspondence about the same subject is filed together (often very convenient).

(*vi*) It eliminates duplication of copies in different departments.

(*vii*) It gives management better control of records.

(*viii*) It helps educate staff with the idea that records are the common property of the business.

(*c*) *Disadvantages.*

(*i*) Lack of departmental knowledge by filing staff.

(*ii*) Delay in files being made available.

(*iii*) The larger the department the easier it is to lose individual records.

(*iv*) There is no opportunity for juniors to learn about filing techniques.

(*v*) It may mean extra staff, if staff is not released in the departments.

12. Indexing. The object of an index is to make it easy to refer to any particular record in a system. Thus sales invoices may be filed numerically, but with an alphabetical index by customers' names maintained, giving the invoice numbers when not known. Forms of index include:

(*a*) book or ordinary page index which is simple and cheap;

(*b*) loose or vertical card index which is always a live index and in the desired order;

(*c*) visible card index which is more expensive but speedier in reference;

(*d*) wheel index which is speedier still for a large volume of records;

(*e*) strip index which is suitable where the information consists of one line of information, such as name and address.

13. Filing equipment. The commonest kinds of equipment in use are box files, lever-arch files, concertina files, vertical filing cabinets and loose-leaf binders (ring, thong and post binders).

Two modern kinds of filing equipment are as follows.

(*a*) *Suspended filing.*

(*i*) Folders or pockets are suspended vertically from metal rods fitted across the inside of the drawers.

(*ii*) Papers are filed in inner folders which are placed inside the suspended pockets, each of which can hold a number of folders.

(*iii*) This system keeps the files upright and tidy, and gives speed of reference by index strips on each pocket.

(*b*) *Lateral filing.*

(*i*) This consists of suspended files with the end of each file in view, bearing the index strip upon it.

(*ii*) Thus lateral files can be taken up to five or six tiers high, saving at least 50 per cent of floor space compared with vertical filing cabinets.

(*iii*) It is also relatively cheaper.

14. Records retention.

(*a*) When filing accommodation is filled, three courses of action are possible:

(*i*) transfer the records to reserve filing (transfer files);

(*ii*) destroy unwanted documents; or

(*iii*) microfilm the documents (and either retain or destroy originals).

(*b*) Because of time taken in "weeding out" records, it is usual to transfer them *en bloc* to reserve filing.

(*c*) Often many unnecessary records are retained and important ones thrown away—hence the need for a retention policy. Moreover, records take up valuable office space and cost money in overhead expenditure.

15. Factors in determining the retention programme.

(a) *The amount of low-cost space available;* if there is plenty, records might be retained for longer periods.

(b) *The volume of individual records;* if it is small, they might also be kept for longer periods.

(c) *Legal requirements:* action is barred on simple contracts after six years and on specialty contracts (under seal) after twelve years. This does not mean that records have to be kept for these periods, but if there is a possibility of legal action (and the goods or services are sufficiently valuable) it would be advisable to keep them.

(d) *Frequency of reference:* how often, i.e. how far back, is reference made to documents? If never beyond one year, then two years' retention might be sufficient.

(e) *A retention programme* would list all the records in the business under headings, "1 year", "2 years", "6 years", "indefinitely", etc., and the factors listed above would be considered jointly. Note that the number of years for which correspondence should be kept depends on its subject matter.

(f) The Historical MS Commission is interested in very old documents which may be of historical interest.

16. Filing of catalogues.

(a) Price lists and catalogues in book form can be filed on shelves in alphabetical order; usually the contents are very varied. This might be supplemented by a card index of subject-matters.

(b) Price lists and sales leaflets are best filed in a suspension filing cabinet, possibly under subject headings or in the same order as the books.

(c) Some system of recording catalogues borrowed is advisable, and they should be dated when received.

(d) If an index is maintained, copious cross-indexing is advisable, including trade names of equipment.

17. Filing of insurance policies.

(a) These are best filed in separate envelopes according to the risk involved: burglary, fire, etc.

(b) The envelopes should be numbered in accordance with an insurance register. On the face of each envelope can be written a summary of the contents.

(c) For safety, the envelopes should be stored in a metal box either in the office safe or at the bank.

(*d*) The register is a list of all the policies in hand, having columns for policy number, premium, due date, risk, property, etc., so that it is not necessary to refer continuously to the policies themselves. The register is an index to the policies whenever reference is required.

NOTE: An advantage of the envelope system of filing is that it facilitates the insertion of endorsement slips, etc.

18. Common faults in filing and records administration.

(*a*) The wrong system of classification has been adopted.

(*b*) Bad organisation and lack of definition of responsibility and authority.

(*c*) Untrained and unsuitable staff.

(*d*) No established filing procedures (e.g. new folders being started without authority, often in duplication).

(*e*) No planned schedules for retention or disposal of records.

(*f*) The space and equipment are inadequate for the purpose.

(*g*) Lack of control over the borrowing of records or their return.

19. Modern techniques.
The capacious memories which are an integral part of word-processing and microcomputer installations store a range of information which is traditionally kept in bulky, often in overcrowded disorder. The Inland Revenue, for example (*see* XXVII, **10**) will accept end of year tax returns on magnetic tape. During the year the individual records "disappear" into the faithful store of the computer handling the payroll.

PROGRESS TEST 28

1. What are the essentials of a good filing system? (**2**)

2. Discuss the relative advantages of alphabetical and numerical systems of filing. (**4, 5**)

3. Name six methods of classification and give examples for the use of each. (**4–9**)

4. What factors must be borne in mind when choosing the appropriate system of classification? (**10**)

5. Discuss the advantages and disadvantages of central filing, and state for which documents it would not be suitable. (**11**)

6. What is meant by indexing? Describe five kinds of index. (**12**)

7. Describe (*a*) suspension files, (*b*) lateral files. (**13**)

8. What factors must be borne in mind when deciding on a programme of retention of office records? **(15)**

9. Why is it important to have a retention policy with office records? **(15)**

10. Describe a method of filing price lists and catalogues. **(16)**

11. Describe a system for filing insurance policies. **(17)**

12. Write a report to the directors recommending improvements in your existing filing systems. **(18)**

CHAPTER XXIX

Microphotography

1. Definition. By means of photographing records at very high speed and at a great reduction in size, microfilming offers great economies in space and storage costs. A typical installation effected recently by a large English company converted 300,000 documents housed in cabinets and boxes requiring space of almost 20 m² into microfilm housed in cabinets occupying only 1 m². A large volume of the paper from which the microfilm is derived is destroyed, and that part which must be retained, e.g. contracts, patents, documents, etc., are transferred to a lower cost area.

Provided that microfilm is correctly indexed and filed (this is more critical than with paper records, as there are no visual clues) it offers much faster retrieval than its paper equivalent. Retrieval of a required record requires only a few seconds after inserting the relevant microfilm into the reader or viewer (these enlarge and project the picture on to a screen for viewing).

2. Technical details.

(*a*) The film used can be 16 mm, 35 mm or 70 mm wide, the largest size being used especially for large plans and drawings.

(*b*) Computer output microfilm (COM).

(*i*) Enables computer-originated data, recorded on magnetic tape, to be converted to alphanumeric information on 16-mm-roll microfilm or 105-mm-wide microfiche.

(*ii*) When enlarged to legible size, the images look like line print-out.

(*iii*) The process is 40 times faster than a line printer, giving 96,000 characters a second.

(*c*) The four main film forms are:

(*i*) rollfilm;

(*ii*) jackets;

(*iii*) microfiche;

(*iv*) aperture cards.

(*d*) Rollfilm is suited to sequentially filed documents which do not need any inserted updating, whereas jackets (15 mm × 10 mm, taking up to 60 images) are useful for easy updating of grouped documents.

(e) Microfiche is a piece of film measuring 15 mm × 10 mm, taking 98 images, and is used where a large number of detailed information has to be accessible at speed to a number of people.

(f) Processed film may also be stored on aperture cards, with an automatic reference coding for fast locating.

(g) The microfilm is mounted in a punched card.

3. Methods of installation.

(a) By installing the full equipment of camera, reader and processing unit. An expensive capital outlay, but justified given a large volume of records.

(b) By installing camera and reader and sending films to the manufacturer for processing.

(c) By installing the reader only and employing a specialist company or firm to microfilm documents and do the processing.

4. Advantages of microfilming.

(a) Considerable saving in filing space.

(b) Safety: important documents can be in safe custody with the company's banker and the microfilm retained for daily consultation.

(c) Solves the "weeding-out" problem. All documents can be microfilmed, then only the few important ones need be retained.

(d) Increase in durability: most film is fire-proof and lasts longer than paper.

(e) It can add to general efficiency of the system.

5. Disadvantages of microfilming.

(a) Reference to records is possible only with the reader and frequent reference may be inconvenient.

(b) Relatively high cost of processing.

(c) Film may sometimes be illegible, usually because of bad filming and processing, or by the use of a wrong reduction ratio (the size of the original to that of the film).

6. Microfilm as legal evidence. The Civil Evidence Act of 1968 provides that microfilm is admissible in evidence if a certificate is given by officers of the company that it was produced by a responsible person in the ordinary course of his employment. The registrar of English companies (at Cardiff) accepts documents, e.g. Annual Returns (required by statute to be filed with him), in microfilm form.

7. New techniques. In common with information storage by other methods, the use of microphotography is likely to decline in the face of the remarkable storage capacity, (and the instantaneous retrieval of data) provided by word-processing and micro-computers.

PROGRESS TEST 29

1. What type of document would you recommend keeping after it has been microfilmed? **(1)**

2. What is the advantage of using a microfiche? **(2)**

3. What is COM? **(2)**

4. What advice would you give to the directors of a company with considerable filing problems but with insufficient capital to purchase a full microfilm installation? **(3)**

5. What major advantages are claimed for microphotography? **(4)**

CHAPTER XXX

Forms: Control and Design

1. Purposes of forms control.

(*a*) To retain only essential forms and to destroy all forms rendered obsolete by changed procedures, amended legislation, etc.

(*b*) To ensure that the essential ones are designed to give greatest efficiency consistent with low cost of production.

(*c*) To produce forms by the most appropriate and low-cost method.

(*i*) Certain forms are imposed by the State, e.g. PAYE system.

(*ii*) Certain minimum standards are required for quoted companies by Stock Exchange regulations.

(*iii*) Where form design is at the discretion of the company the method of production is ideally provided by the printing department of the large company itself.

(*iv*) The smaller company has to place orders outside and the utmost care is necessary in a notoriously expensive market.

(*d*) To distribute forms only to the departments requiring them: the issue of forms requires as great a control as that required for the issue of stationery.

(*e*) To review periodically all forms in use to ensure their continuing relevance to the office systems.

(*f*) To evaluate forms primarily on the time required to understand them, to fill them in and use them.

2. Initiating forms control.

Effective forms control consists of the setting up at head office of a single office or department (which may be an O & M department) whose function is to achieve the above purposes.

The following basic steps are necessary to set up forms control.

(*a*) Inform all staff that forms control will operate from the date stated. The function and authority of the official or department is clearly defined.

(*b*) Freeze all forms activity; all form requests to be made to the forms office.

(*c*) Compile a "forms file" with specimens of every form, both "home-made" and statutory, used in the company.

(*d*) Classify the forms and compile a "forms register".

(*e*) Briefly summarise on each form in the register the method of its use. This method is useful in training clerks.

(*f*) Standardise forms wherever possible in size, colour and weight of paper (a material factor when posting forms).

3. Common faults in form design.

(*a*) Too complicated: simplicity must be the aim in good design.

(*b*) Of the wrong shape to fit existing filing system.

(*c*) Requiring too much writing: much standard material can be pre-printed on the form.

(*d*) Superfluous, or duplicating other forms.

(*e*) Using paper of a quality too good for the job, thereby incurring unnecessary expense.

(*f*) Failing to take advantage of different colours of paper to promote rapid recognition and filing.

(*g*) In the absence of effective control, heads of department, foremen, etc., start their own records and design their own forms.

(*h*) Many forms are scrapped when the system is modified, although a minor alteration to the form might retain its usefulness. The system of overprinting the old forms is cheaper than scrapping them and ordering expensive new ones.

4. Systems and forms.
The interrelationship between the system and the forms which it generates and uses is so close that it is not easy to ask which came first. As an office expands in the scope and complexity of its work the need for expert O & M study becomes urgent. Many systems grow spontaneously and generate forms which may well exhibit many of the faults described in **3**. Since O & M usually leads to a revision of the system, revision of forms is a necessary consequence.

5. New techniques.
Word-processing and microcomputers have a profound effect on the design and use of forms in the automated office. The manufacturers of the many types of devices on the market advise a company's own O & M team about form design adapted to the needs of the office and to the installation of the processors. The retention and retrieval of large volumes of data by and from the capacious memories of microprocessors and word-processors achieve economies in paper: the traditional form with its carbon copies is replaced by a permanent, instantly retrievable impulse on the floppy disc or other medium in the store.

PROGRESS TEST 30

1. In what cases does the company have no control over the design of forms? **(1)**

2. What are the major purposes of forms control? **(1)**

3. Why is standardisation of forms an important element of design? **(2)**

4. Give an example, preferably from your own experience of bad form design. **(3)**

5. What part does colour play in form production? **(3)**

6. Give an example of efficient form design, either by reference to this chapter xxvii or from your own experience, submitting reasons for your belief in its merits.

7. Discuss the likely effect on forms use and designs of the proposal for a fully-automated office. **(5)**

CHAPTER XXXI

Communications

1. Introduction. Communication is the act of imparting information. Failure to impart the right information to the right person at the right time is one of the major causes of inefficiency.

Office communications can be classified as follows.

(a) *Telephone* (oral); external and internal.
(b) *Written*; letters by post and messenger service.
(c) *Mechanical*:
    (i) teleprinter (and telex);
    (ii) facsimile telegraphy;
    (iii) pneumatic tube;
    (iv) television.
(d) *Staff location systems*, which may be by:
    (i) sound;
    (ii) public address system;
    (iii) light signals; or
    (iv) radio.

2. Factors to consider when choosing type of communications.

(a) *Urgency of message:* therefore degree of speed.
(b) *Accuracy of message:* writing in some form is usually preferable to the oral form.
(c) *Secrecy:* can the information be kept confidential from all except the addressee? (consider in this context the use of commercial codes, e.g. Bentley's code).
(d) *Recording of message:* note the practical importance of carbon copies of letters.
(e) *Impression made on customers:* e.g. the practice of selling by telephone.
(f) *Cost of specialised equipment:* e.g. private data terminal equipment, and running costs.
(g) *Convenience in use to the sender.*
(h) *Need for trained staff:* e.g. switchboard operators.
(i) *Distance:* practical limitations of communication by some types.

3. Telephone systems.

(*a*) *Direct exchange line service with extensions.*

(*i*) This is a telephone fitted with switches connected to another telephone (*see* Table XI):

TABLE XI: Operation of Direct Line Telephone with Extension.

Switch no.	Result
1	Speak to exchange
2	Speak to extension (caller cannot hear)
3	Transfer exchange to extension
4	Normal intercommunication between the two instruments

(*ii*) It enables a private secretary to screen calls for an executive.

(*iii*) It is a method of supplying a telephone to an office with little outgoing traffic.

(*b*) *"Keymaster" system.*

(*i*) Each instrument is fitted with buttons representing five or ten extensions and one or two exchange lines.

(*ii*) Dialling facilities can be given or withheld from extensions as desired.

(*iii*) No switchboard is necessary.

(*c*) *PMBX* (Private Manual Branch Exchange).

(*i*) Entails the use of a switchboard and operator; the board may be cord or lever operated.

(*ii*) With a PMBX the operator makes all connections between extensions as well as connecting outgoing and incoming calls.

(*d*) *PABX* (Private Automatic Branch Exchange).

(*i*) Similar to a PMBX except that each internal telephone instrument has its own dial and extensions can dial one another as well as outgoing calls.

(*ii*) A switchboard operator is still required to route incoming calls, but in large installations it does reduce the number of operators required.

(*iii*) Some modern switchboards are push-button.

(*iv*) Such a switchboard can be bought from private manufacturers instead of from British Telecom.

(*e*) *PBX* (Private Branch Exchange, or private telephone system).

(*i*) An internal telephone system, which may have a switchboard, and gives automatic button or dial connection between extensions.

(*ii*) It is not connected to the national telephone system at all.

(*f*) *Executive (or loudspeaker) systems.*

(*i*) The executive's telephone, although not usually the other instruments, is fitted with a loudspeaker.

(*ii*) The executive is frequently given priority of call, ability to speak to several extensions at once, and a light signal as well as (or instead of) a bell or buzzer.

NOTE: Complete loudspeaking telephone systems are now available in which all instruments are fitted with loudspeakers.

4. Choosing a telephone system. Apart from a house exchange system (suitable for a small business) the main choice lies between installing a complete PABX throughout the business, or a PMBX combined with some internal telephone system such as an internal PBX.

The main deciding factor will be the ratio of internal calls compared with external calls at different extensions. If all extensions require outgoing facilities, then a PABX will be advisable (PMBX in smaller concerns). If a large proportion of the extensions only need internal communication, then consideration should be given to a PMBX with a PBX or some other internal telephone system.

(*a*) *PABX advantages.*

(*i*) All calls can be made automatically.

(*ii*) Only one telephone to answer.

(*iii*) It may be cheaper in large concerns.

(*b*) *PABX disadvantages.* Loss of control over outgoing calls.

(*c*) *PMBX and PBX advantages.*

(*i*) May be cheaper if there are fewer telephone operators.

(*ii*) Gives a better control over calls.

(*d*) *PMBX and PBX disadvantages.*

(*i*) If PMBX, manual connections.

(*ii*) Two telephones on desk—more noise.

5. Telephone charges. The introduction of subscriber trunk dialling (STD) has greatly increased the speed and improved the convenience of the telephone. The STD call charges from ordinary (non-coinbox) Lines (VAT exclusive) are based on a fixed charge per unit as defined in the *Post Office Guide*. The many telephone services available include Freefone for subscribers who wish their customers or agents to make calls to them without payment.

6. Telephone answering machines. Special machines can be connected to the telephone which will:

(*a*) answer the call (if it is not otherwise answered in 10 seconds); and

(*b*) record any message dictated by the caller.

(*c*) The messages are recorded on magnetic tape which can be played back subsequently and typed out.

(*d*) One hour's dictation or more is obtainable on the machines.

(*e*) Such a machine is useful:

(*i*) when telephone orders are frequently received (a special telephone number can be allocated and notified to customers); and

(*ii*) because urgent requests at any time of the day or night can be recorded;

(*iii*) it can save the time of staff when used during the day;

(*iv*) it is useful for sales representatives to record their latest orders.

7. Radio-telephones. These are used when it is wished to keep in touch with, e.g. ships, although the service from aircraft is available in the direction air to ground only.

8. Written communications.

(*a*) *Normal Post Office services*, including:

(*i*) registered letters;

(*ii*) special delivery service;

(*iii*) railway and airway letters;

(*iv*) airmail;

(*v*) cash on delivery (c.o.d.) service;

(*vi*) recorded delivery;

(*vii*) business reply service;

(*viii*) express services, including railex and Post Office messenger services;

(*ix*) telegrams—note sender's special instructions, e.g. confidential, may be written on the envelope in which the telegram is delivered;

(*x*) Giro services.

(*b*) *Teleprinters.*

(*c*) *Telex.*

(*d*) *Facsimile telegraphy.*

(*e*) *Confravision.*

(*f*) *Datel services.*

9. Teleprinters. A teleprinter resembles a typewriter, and is easily operated by a typist after a little practice.

(*a*) It is connected to a telephone line, and messages typed at one end are simultaneously reproduced on the machine at the other end.

(*b*) Teleprinters are rented from British Telecom and form part of the private telecommunication services.

(*c*) British Telecom provides modulators/demodulators (modems) to enable private data terminal equipment to be used.

(*d*) Private modems, conforming to British Telecom requirements, may be used to provide means of transmitting and receiving data over private circuits.

10. Telex. The telex service provides a fast means of printed communication, a copy of the message being produced on teleprinters at both the sending and receiving installations.

(*a*) The United Kingdom telex service is fully automatic and immediate connection is made by direct dialling to any subscriber in this country.

(*b*) Messages may be sent to, or received by, a subscriber even though his teleprinter is unattended (for example at night); this facility is particularly useful on overseas calls where there may be a difference between local times or office hours.

11. Facsimile telegraphy. This is a means of transmitting written (as opposed to typed) messages, although pre-typed messages can be transmitted.

(*a*) Messages are sent over a private wire or even over British Telecom telephone wire to a similar receiving machine at a distance.

(*b*) Developments of this kind of machine now make it possible even to send messages across the Atlantic in this way.

(*c*) It requires no special operator and enables not only handwritten messages but also drawings, formulae, etc., to be transmitted quickly from place to place.

(*d*) A 200 mm × 280 mm document can be transmitted in 10 minutes.

12. Confravision. This is a British Telecom service which links groups of people in distant locations in sound and vision.

(*a*) The facilities (at studios in London, Birmingham, Bristol, Glasgow and Manchester) are all customer controlled.

(*b*) The system is designed to allow meetings to be effectively conducted as though the participants were face to face.

(*c*) Any two or three studios can be simultaneously interconnected.

13. Datel services. These are services providing for digital data transmission.

(*a*) Data prepared in any five-unit code on punched paper tape may be transmitted over the telex network or leased telegraph circuits.

(*b*) Automatic error detection equipment can be provided if required.

(*c*) The digital data signals can be converted for transmission over speech circuits, and vice-versa, using modems.

(*d*) There is a very wide range of datel services, e.g. the Datel 2400 Dial Up Service provides facilities for simultaneous two-way transmissions of data over four-wire leased circuits at a speed of 2400 bits per second.

14. Mechanical means of communication.

(*a*) Staff location systems.

(*b*) Pneumatic tube installations.

(*c*) Conveyors and gravity chutes.

(*d*) The punched-card "auto-route" system (only used in the factory so far).

15. Staff locating systems. It is often useful to be able to contact important executives immediately, and there are four main methods of doing so.

(*a*) *Loudspeaker system.*

(*i*) The telephone operator usually has the microphone, and messages can be relayed all over the business premises simultaneously.

(*ii*) It is useful in noisy factories.

(*iii*) If used consistently can be very noisy and disturbing to the workers.

(*b*) *Bells and buzzers.*

(*i*) These usually have a code of long and short "rings", used to indicate different executives.

(*ii*) They are possibly better than loudspeakers but still disturbing to workers.

(*c*) *Light signals.*

(*i*) The signs have large 5-cm, 10-cm or 15-cm figures with lights behind them (or behind figures on a clock).

(*ii*) Again, a code of different combinations of the figures denotes different people being called.

(*iii*) They are quieter than (*a*) or (*b*) but the light signals are not always seen and, in fact, can be ignored.

(*d*) *Radio call system.*

(*i*) A central transmitter is located usually with the telephone operator.

(*ii*) Different wavelengths are allocated for different executives, each of whom carries a portable radio receiver.

(*iii*) When a call is transmitted for a certain person, only that person receives the call, and it continues until he answers a telephone and announces his availability.

(*iv*) This system has the advantage that no noise disturbs other workers: only the person called is aware of the call, and he cannot ignore it.

(*v*) However, it is more expensive to install.

16. Pneumatic tube system.

(*a*) Tubing is installed, connecting different departments, and documents are placed in containers which are sucked along the tubes by electrically induced suction.

(*b*) Speed can be as high as 10 m per second.

(*c*) Pneumatic tubing can be obtained which gives automatic routing to the department required.

(*d*) The method is very useful where speed is essential or where messenger staff are expensive or difficult to obtain.

(*e*) It is the fastest way of sending actual documents from one office to another.

17. Conveyors and gravity chutes.

(*a*) Slow-moving conveyors have been installed in offices and are useful to ensure a continuous flow of work from one worker to another.

(*b*) Gravity chutes are useful where documents (or parcels) are frequently sent from an upper to a lower floor.

18. Television.

(*a*) In recent years there have been developments in closed-circuit television for business purposes.

(*b*) It offers the advantage of being able to show on the screen to a caller in another office (say) a page from a ledger without having to send it to the office concerned.

(*c*) Some banks have installed television for this purpose.

19. Prestel. The British Telecom Prestel/Viewdata computer-based

information system is the most comprehensive visual communications system in the world today (August 1981). Prestel is based on a bank of linked computers situated in various parts of the British Isles. Its full potential is not yet realised but it is rapidly developing. It offers the user almost limitless information of general and particular nature on every usual subject, project or company—a super encyclopaedia, surely.

Prestel/Viewdata operates on an interaction of three main elements, a modified television set, a telephone connection and a battery of linked computers. The system has great potential for "closed-user" information services, availability being restricted to users having the necessary access code given by the information provider. Information instantly available includes:

(a) Up-to-the minute stock market situation;
(b) Public company financial results;
(c) economic statistics.

Prestel linked hard-copy printers make a permanent record of a Prestel transmission for future reference, copying and distribution. Users may advertise on it and order direct through the system using credit cards or previously arranged credit facilities.

PROGRESS TEST 31

1. What major factors should be considered when choosing communications? (2)

2. An executive in your company prefers to use the telephone to writing a letter. Discuss the pros and cons. (2)

3. State the advantages of (a) PABX; (b) PMBX and PBX. (4)

4. What are the major Post Office services relating to written communications? (8)

5. What is the basic difference between teleprinters and telex? (9, 10)

6. Describe a method whereby complicated plans and drawings can be transmitted from one office to another with minimum delay. (11)

7. What is Confravision? (12)

8. What are Datel services? (13)

9. What are the major types of staff locating systems? (15)

10. What is Prestel? (19)

CHAPTER XXXII

Inward Mail

1. Importance of the inward mail. Inward mail is normally the major input into the office system, generating and maintaining its activities. Staff handling it must not only arrive before the main office work begins (this may complicate flexible working hours), but include responsible clerks in view of the fact that cash in various forms is often included in the mail.

2. Basic procedure. The following basic steps are common to most systems.

(*a*) Certain clerks (supervised by a senior), should attend about half an hour to an hour before the office opens, so that the mail can be distributed by the time other clerks arrive.

(*b*) The intial sorting is into non-registered mail and registered mail. The latter is recorded in a special register and opened only by the supervisor.

(*c*) The second sorting is into:

    (*i*) private and urgent mail;

    (*ii*) sealed envelopes;

    (*iii*) unsealed envelopes.

Clerks handling mail should be trained in the skill of rapid sorting of documents.

(*d*) *Cheques, money orders, postal orders, girocheques, etc., and cash.*

    (*i*) All remittances coming in must be checked with remittance advices, monthly statements, etc., which are ticked and initialled if found to be correct.

    (*ii*) If they are incorrect, the fact should be reported at once to the supervisor.

    (*iii*) If any cheques are found to be uncrossed, the supervisor should at once cross them.

    (*iv*) Cash should be listed and totalled, then passed to the cashier, who should give a receipt for it.

(*e*) Rubber-stamp all letters and other documents with the

time and date of receipt in the top right-hand corner, or on the back of the document (if there is no room on the front).

(*f*) Check all enclosures and attach them to the letter or other document (failure to do this is a common source of confusion and time-wasting).

(*g*) Letters which quote the company's own reference, e.g. ABC/DE, will be sorted by department of destination; the supervisor will decide the distribution of letters whose destination is uncertain.

(*h*) Sort letters according to departments using appropriate sorting devices such as flap sorters, pigeon-holes, etc.

(*i*) *Always* check "empty" envelopes to ensure that nothing has been left inside.

(*j*) Distribute mail as quickly as possible after it has been received: delay may be dangerous.

(*k*) Organise a messenger service to distribute mail to the departments. Note the pneumatic tube system or conveyors and gravity chutes explained in XXXI, **16**, **17**, to deal with large quantities of mail and parcels.

(*l*) Ensure that internal check is adequately applied to money receipts in their many forms. Note also the importance of correspondence containing confidential information; only the supervisor should be responsible for delivery of these.

3. Machines and equipment.

(*a*) *Letter-opening machines*, which slice off a narrow strip from the side of the envelope. This should be used with caution, for it is easy to cut a strip also off the contents.

(*b*) *Date stamp*, to be applied immediately to every document. This will impress the time and the date and suitable wording on the document.

(*c*) *Sorting equipment*. Suspension files may be necessary for a large volume of mail, although the conventional pigeon-hole method is widely used in smaller companies. Flap sorters save desk space.

4. Letters for the attention of different departments. There are several methods of dealing with this common situation.

(*a*) Simply write in pencil at the top of letter the names of persons or departments who should see it (this chore often gets overlooked).

(*b*) Stick on an adhesive label bearing the same information and a space for the initials of the people who are to see the document (the label is more easily seen).

(*c*) Institute the use of a rubber stamp incorporating the initials of all the members of a department and mark which ones should see each letter, again with a signature column (but there is not always room for such a stamp).

(*d*) Use a photocopying machine to make several copies of the incoming letter; distribute the original to the person having to take action, and photocopies to other persons concerned (there is no delay, and the other persons receive the information the same day).

PROGRESS TEST 32

1. On what grounds would you recommend that dealing with inward mail is introduced early in the training of commercial trainees? **(1)**

2. How should registered mail be dealt with? **(2)**

3. What kind of internal check would you apply to the receipt of cash, cheques, etc.? **(2)**

4. Why is the use of a date stamp important? **(2)**

5. Describe the methods available for sorting a large volume of inward mail. **(2, 3)**

6. In what circumstances is a photocopying machine useful in handling inward mail? **(4)**

CHAPTER XXXIII

Outward Mail

1. Introduction. There are advantages even in a small business in routing all outgoing mail through one person or department. It:

    (*a*) fixes responsibility;

    (*b*) controls the use of postage stamps;

    (*c*) develops experts in postage rates.

The recent big increases in the cost of postal services render imperative an O & M investigation into the modernisation of a company's mail room.

2. Outward mail procedure. The detailed procedure will vary with the size of the business and the volume of outgoing mail, but the following are the usual steps involved.

    (*a*) Decide where envelopes are to be typed at the time of typing the letter, or centrally (usually the former).

    (*b*) Give instructions that letters requiring the special attention of the post clerk, e.g. first class, registered, foreign, etc., should be marked in pencil in the top right-hand corner to that effect.

    (*c*) Institute regular collection of mail from the departments where it is signed. Regular collection during the day will help to relieve congestion at the end of the day.

    (*d*) Fix a deadline at the end of the day after which letters will not be accepted for dispatch that day (without special permission from a designated official).

    (*e*) Ensure that the post clerk deals methodically with the post and sorts it into "home" and "overseas" and into different denominations before stamping. If there is more than one piece of paper in a letter, it should be weighed to ensure that the right amount of postage is affixed.

    (*f*) Use folding and sealing machines when large quantities of letters are to be posted.

    (*g*) To avoid letters being placed in the wrong envelopes, window envelopes could be used.

    (*h*) Write brief details of all letters in the post book (possibly not so important when franking machines are used: *see* **4** below).

(*i*) Instruct the post clerk to check all "Encs" on letters and to see that enclosures are actually attached.

(*j*) Decide on the method of stamping (*see* **3** below).

(*k*) If a franking machine is used it should be returned to the office safe each night.

(*l*) The post book should be kept on the imprest system to prevent fraud.

(*i*) Balance the post book every day.

(*ii*) Prohibit sale of stamps to employees.

(*m*) Instruct the office staff that the office post must not be used for private mail.

(*n*) All Post Office receipts for registered and recorded delivery letters and parcels to be gummed in the special book provided.

(*o*) Always state the post code on envelopes, where this is known.

3. Stamping and posting. There are four main methods of stamping.

(*a*) Purchase of sheets of adhesive stamps from the post office. They should be kept in special folders and detached for daily use (but stamps are apt to get lost, and the method is time-consuming when checking stocks of stamps).

(*b*) Use of stamp-emitting machine (can be hired) which gives a meter check on the number used and in stock.

(*i*) Separate machines are required for each denomination.

(*ii*) Refill stamps can be purchased in rolls from the Post Office.

(*c*) Use of franking machine (*see* **4** below).

(*d*) By pre-payment at the Post Office.

(*i*) The number of letters must be at least 120.

(*ii*) The number of parcels must be at least 20.

(*iii*) The Post Office will then frank letters on cheque-payment of the postage incurred.

4. Franking machines. A postal franker is a machine purchased privately from the manufacturers, who first have to obtain a licence in the buyer's name from the Post Office.

(*a*) A lever on the machine is set for the rate of postage desired.

(*b*) When operated (manually or electrically) the machine prints on the envelope a representation of a postage stamp and the date cancellation mark.

(*c*) Before the machine can be used, advance payment has to be made to the local Post Office for the value of stamps it is expected to use, when a meter is set on the machine for that amount.

(*d*) When the amount has been used up, the machine locks and has to be taken back to the Post Office for a further payment.

(*e*) The machine records on a dial the total postage used and, on bigger machines, the amount of postage unused as well.

(*f*) The mail has to be taken to the Post Office and a Post Office form has to be completed with the number of letters of different denominations put through the machine.

(*g*) *Advantages.*

(*i*) *Great speed* is obtained (2000 an hour on a hand-operated machine and up to 15,000 an hour on an automatic electric one).

(*ii*) *Safety.* It eliminates the use of loose stamps.

(*iii*) *Accounting control.* The dials on the machine provide an accurate record.

(*iv*) *Advertising value.* As it franks, the machine can simultaneously print the Company name on all outgoing mail.

(*v*) *Convenience.* The manufacturers claim that it eliminates the need for keeping a post book.

(*vi*) *Dispatch of mail.* Since the letters are already franked, they are not held up by the Post Office for official franking.

(*vii*) *It can save printing costs* on envelopes, e.g. instead of an advertising slogan a rubric such as "If undelivered please return to X Co. Ltd" can be printed.

(*h*) *Disadvantages.*

(*i*) Juniors may waste postage by franking wrong amounts on letters (through failing to adjust the machine).

(*ii*) It is suitable only for a large outgoing mail.

(*iii*) Letters have to be taken to the Post Office, which may be some distance from the office.

(*iv*) It may be argued that it does not eliminate the need for keeping a post book, since it gives no record of *what* letters have been sent out, only the number and postage value.

(*v*) Even with a franking machine, it may still be necessary to have loose stamps for receipts, urgent letters and letters to be posted when the Post Office is closed.

(*i*) Franking machines must be leased or purchased from one of three specified supplying companies (*Post Office Guide*, November 1980, page 59), authorised by the Post Office.

5. Machines and equipment.

(*a*) Franking machines.

(*b*) Letter openers.

(*c*) Folder/inserters.

(*d*) Collators.

(*e*) Addresser printers.

(*f*) Letter openers for incoming mail, which may well be handled in the central mail room.

(*g*) Letter and parcel scales.

(*h*) The up-to-date official *Post Office Guide*.

(*i*) Brown paper, corrugated cardboard, sellotape, sealing-wax, string.

(*j*) In view of the frequent congestion of mail-room activities, the layout of the office must be carefully planned.

6. Business Reply system. This Post Office service enables a business to send out unstamped reply cards or leaflets which the recipients can mail back to the original sender without having to pay postage.

(*a*) It is greatly used for soliciting business, guarantee cards, etc.

(*b*) The business makes itself responsible for the postal charges on all replies received.

(*c*) Arrangements for printing the cards and the cost of doing so must also be borne by the business.

(*d*) The user of the service may also incorporate in his advertisements in newspapers, trade journals, etc., one of the special business reply designs, to be used as an address label or a folder.

(*e*) Folders, however, are outside the preferred (POP) range and may therefore attract additional postage as non-POP items.

(*f*) Designs are available for first- and second-class mail, and must state the licence number of the licensee.

(*g*) Post Office requirements.

(*i*) A licence must first be obtained from the local Head Postmaster.

(*ii*) A deposit must be paid in advance sufficient to cover the amount of the charges likely to accrue during a period of approximately a month.

(*iii*) When the sum so paid is nearly exhausted, the licensee must renew his credit by a further payment.

(*iv*) In addition he must pay an annual fee of £15.

(*v*) The cards, in envelopes, etc., must conform to a pattern laid down by the Post Office: cards must not be less than 100 mm long × 70 mm wide.

(*vi*) The name and address of the business must be printed below the panel containing the licence number.

(*vii*) "No postage required if posted in Great Britain or Northern Ireland" must be printed in the top right-hand corner.

(*viii*) "Postage will be paid by the licensee" must be printed in the top left-hand corner.

(*ix*) There must be two wide black vertical lines near the right-hand edge.

(*x*) The cards or leaflets returned by the recipients are then delivered to the licensee through the post in the normal way.

(*xi*) A charge of $\frac{1}{2}$p for each one in addition to normal postage is then due.

(*xii*) Against this the deposit previously paid is offset.

(*g*) The first and second class designs appear on pp. 46–47 in the *Post Office Guide*, November 1980.

(*h*) In addition to the Business Reply Service, the Post Office offers the Freepost Service. A person who wishes to obtain a reply from a client or member of the public without putting him to the expense of paying postage may include in his communication or advertisement a special address. The reply bearing this address can then be posted in the ordinary way but without a stamp and the addressee will pay postage on all the replies that he receives. (The replies may be sent only as second class mail.) An annual fee (August 1981) of £15 per licence or extension to a licence is payable by the addressee to the Post Office.

7. Remitting money through the post.

(*a*) *By cheque.* Perhaps most convenient and giving greatest security. Note the alternatives of traders' credit and credit transfer.

(*b*) *By postal order.* Suitable for small amounts and where the recipient may not have a bank account.

(*c*) *By sending notes and coins* in a registered envelope. The envelope must be of the special strong type supplied by the Post Office, or similar to it. This method is suitable only for the payment of very small amounts. Nothing intended for registration should be dropped into a letter-box. This method is costly, and wherever possible payment should be effected by the use of a crossed cheque.

(*d*) The National Giro Service provides a low cost current account banking and money transfer service in which accounts are held centrally at National Giro, Bootle, Merseyside.

8. Urgent letters.
It is useful in business to know the different methods of sending letters quickly: the following alternatives are available.

(*a*) *Full express service*. A charge is made of so much per km according to the distance sent (the most expensive but suitable for short distances).

(*b*) *Special delivery* (also known as Express). The Post Office arranges for the letter to be specially delivered from the Post Office in the area of the addressee, i.e. before the normal delivery service.

(*c*) *Railway letter*. By arrangement with the Post Office, first-class letters can be handed in at railway stations and will be sent by the next train to the station at the destination, either:

(*i*) to be called for, or

(*ii*) to be put in the post locally.

Envelopes must be marked accordingly.

(*d*) From 1st July 1981, British Rail no longer offers any parcel delivery service. In future Royal Mail Parcel Services, will be operated which are precisely designed for local, regional or national individual needs. The services include:

(*i*) Datapost;

(*ii*) Expresspost;

(*iii*) Direct Bag;

(*iv*) Nightrider, for over-night contract delivery within the London area;

(*v*) County Parcels service;

(*vi*) Local Delivery Contract Service, to take goods short distances overnight.

(*e*) *Late posting*. This service is available only for first-class letters.

NOTE: Rates of postage have been purposely omitted because of changes in rates from time to time; for these, reference should be made to the current edition of the *Post Office Guide*.

(*g*) *Datapost*. This provides a highly reliable, door-to-door, over overnight delivery service.

(*i*) Packages are collected from customers at agreed times.

(*ii*) They are delivered the next working morning, again at agreed times.

(*iii*) For an annual fee, the customer can use the service when required.

9. Private boxes. Note that there is available a private box for inward post, and a private *posting* box for outward post.

(*a*) *Private box.*

(*i*) A private box can be rented from the Post Office for the reception or delivery of postal packets, as an alternative to delivery.

(*ii*) It is thus possible to obtain delivery before the normal delivery services.

(*iii*) Letters must include the box number in the address.

(*iv*) Rental must be paid 12 months in advance.

(*v*) If delivery is required between 6 a.m. and the start of the first delivery, double fees are payable.

(*vi*) The service is useful for quoting box numbers in advertisements and when advertising for staff. All the mail is accumulated until it is required, and it avoids callers worrying the office.

(*b*) *Private posting box.*

(*i*) This is installed at the entrance to the premises of the business concern, for the posting of letters.

(*ii*) An initial fee is payable, which is renewable every 12 months.

(*c*) *Lockable private bag.*

(*i*) This facility is for the posting and receipt of correspondence.

(*ii*) The bag is conveyed to and from the post office by the user or by a postman (for an additional fee).

(*iii*) The bag and key are supplied by the user.

NOTE: Where there are at least 1000 items (or postage exceeds £10) the Post Office will arrange a special free collection.

10. Recorded delivery.

(*a*) This in an alternative to registered post, and is a much cheaper form of obtaining proof of postage.

(*b*) For extra payment, proof of delivery can also be obtained.

(*c*) It is not to be used for sending cash but is useful for sending important documents through the post.

(*d*) Compensation is limited to £2, which is much lower than with registered post.

PROGRESS TEST 33

1. Why may there be an urgent need to modernise a company's mail room? **(1)**

2. State three routine precautions you would take before posting letters. **(2)**

3. What are the major advantages of franking machines? **(4)**

4. You are about to equip a mail room. State the requirements, other than machines, which you would consider indispensable. **(5)**

5. What facilities are there for urgent letters? **(8)**

6. What important service offered by British Rail is no longer available? **(8)**

7. What are private boxes and bags and what are their advantages? **(9)**

8. What is recorded delivery? For what purposes would you *not* use it? **(10)**

CHAPTER XXXIV

The Art of Correspondence

1. The importance of correspondence. Letters form a substantial volume of the exports of many offices. If they are:

(*a*) well typed;

(*b*) well drafted (avoiding business jargon);

(*c*) relevant;

(*d*) sent as soon as possible in reply to the corresponding inward mail;

they play an important part in preserving the goodwill of the company among its customers and its image among the public in general.

2. Cost of correspondence. Letter writing is, however, an expensive function of the office and unnecessary time and technique given to it add to the variable costs of the office.

The elements of cost include the following.

(*a*) *Salaries* of the dictator, typist, filing clerk, messenger, etc.

(*b*) *Stationery:* letterhead (bond), carbon copies (bank), envelopes and carbons.

(*c*) *Equipment:* typewriters, dictating machines, cassettes, etc.

(*d*) *Stamps* and work of stamping or franking.

(*e*) *Waste* resulting from spoiled stationery, loss of stamps, etc.

(*f*) *Overhead expenditure:* rent, rates, insurance, etc. The total cost of sending one letter is often surprisingly high—£10 is not an uncommon estimate.

3. Control of correspondence. Efficient office administration includes the task of getting *necessary* letters *well written* and to prevent the writing of unnecessary ones.

The major methods of control include the following.

(*a*) By heads of departments signing all outgoing letters (a popular method). On no account must any clerk other than the head, or person expressly authorised by him, sign letters.

(*b*) By regular monthly conferences to criticise letters sent out and to suggest improvements in style and presentation.

(*c*) By the use of form letters.

4. Methods of answering letters.

(*a*) Dictating to a shorthand typist or a cassette or other dictating machine device.

(*b*) Dictating some paragraphs and using form (standard) paragraphs for the remainder.

(*c*) Using complete form letters (*see* **6** below).

(*d*) Drafting letters in writing (manuscripts) and passing them to a copy-typist. This is appropriate only for important matters or legal correspondence.

(*e*) Jotting down the gist of the reply and leaving a private secretary to compose the letter.

(*f*) Entrusting a secretary to compose the entire letter.

(*g*) Writing the reply on the bottom of each incoming letter and sending a photocopy of it.

(*h*) By word-processing. This is the automatic or semi-automatic manipulation of text by electronic means, and the automatic production of first-time final copy. Modern word-processing systems are of two types:

(*i*) stand-alone or independent systems; and

(*ii*) centralised or shared-logic systems.

An inherent factor in installing these systems is the breakup of the traditional executive/secretary relationship.

5. The technique of letter-writing. The test of a business letter is whether it clearly expresses what the writer has to say, so that it is equally clearly understood.

The basic rules of writing letters are as follows.

(*a*) Be brief, without being curt, using short words and sentences. Correct punctuation is important.

(*b*) Be friendly, without being familiar.

(*c*) Be sincere and not florid, avoiding gobbledygook, i.e. involved phrases tending to confuse rather than enlighten.

(*d*) Be as tactful as the occasion requires, e.g. be direct, without being rude, when pressing for money.

(*e*) Avoid like the plague the use of so-called "business English", e.g. do not write "I am in receipt of your letter and thank you for same": write instead "Thank you for your letter".

6. Form letters (or cards). These are standardised letters used by a business to answer all correspondence of a similar and recurring nature and to give the same information to all correspondents, e.g. debt collection letters, acknowledgments or applications for employment, order acknowledgments, etc.

(*a*) *Initiating form letters.*

(*i*) For several weeks make extra copies of all outgoing letters.

(*ii*) At the end of the period sort the letters by subject-matter.

(*iii*) Determine the types of letter most frequently written and the most frequently used paragraphs.

(*iv*) Select the best reply to each and if possible improve on it.

(*v*) Standardise and incorporate them into form letters or form paragraphs.

(*vi*) Repeat the procedure every 12 months to keep up-to-date.

(*b*) *Advantages of form letters.*

(*i*) They ensure uniform practice in letter-writing.

(*ii*) They save the time of both dictator and typists.

(*iii*) They assist in speedy answering of correspondence.

(*c*) *Disadvantages* of form letters.

(*i*) They are not sympathetic to individual cases.

(*ii*) The style of the letter may be officious and pompous.

(*iii*) Printed letters are not given so much attention by the recipient as personally typed letters.

(*iv*) Form letters quickly become out of date.

7. Reducing costs of correspondence.

(*a*) Use form letters (or cards) wherever possible.

(*b*) Use dictating machines.

(*c*) Use window envelopes.

(*d*) Use a franking machine.

(*e*) Use the telephone instead of writing a letter. It is often cheaper to do so and queries can often be settled in a few minutes.

PROGRESS TEST 34

1. Examine the elements of cost incurred in drafting a letter thanking a correspondent for some useful information.   (**2**)

2. What method of control would you recommend to ensure that all incoming mail is answered as quickly as possible, or otherwise satisfactorily accounted for?   (**3**)

3. What is "word-processing"?   (**4**)

4. An executive has the habit of writing his reply on the bottom of each incoming letter and asking his secretary to send a photocopy of it. Discuss the merits and demerits of this habit.   (**4**)

5. What are the major criteria by which the merits of a business letter should be assessed?   (**5**)

6. What is a form letter? What steps would you take to minimise its disadvantages? **(6)**

7. Discuss the advantages and possible disadvantages of telephoning rather than writing a letter. **(7)**

CHAPTER XXXV

Stationery Control

1. The importance of effective stationery control. Stationery includes both headed and blank paper, bound books, typewriter ribbons, pencils, rubbers, paper clips, tags, etc. The cost of stationery, especially that of paper, has greatly increased in recent years and unless a rigorous check is maintained on the buying, storing, issue and use of it, the variable costs of a department will be unnecessarily heavy.

The essentials of control are:

(*a*) Checking what is ordered.

(*b*) Buying in economical quantities. Note the ICI formula for determining the optimum ordering quantity (Q) in order to minimise the total acquisition cost (ordering + storage):

$$Q = \sqrt{(200Ao)/s}$$

In this formula A is the annual requirement (in units or in value of the particular stationery involved), o is the cost (in £s) of placing and chasing one order for it, and s is the percentage of the value of the average quantity in stock which it costs to store it. For example, a certain office uses 1,000 boxes of envelopes per annum. The O & M department reports that the cost of placing and chasing one order is £9 and that the cost of storage is 10 per cent of the value of the average quantity in store. What is the optimum ordering quantity Q?

$$Q = \sqrt{(200 \times 1,000 \times 9)/10} = 424 \text{ boxes.}$$

The total acquisition cost per annum—which is a minimum—is therefore:

Cost of ordering = 1,000/424 × £9 =	£21.20
Storage cost = 424/2 × 0.1 =	£21.20
Total acquisition cost −	£42.40

(*c*) Using the best buying technique.

(*d*) Avoid over-stocking. Paper, in particular, tends to deteriorate with time and sizes may become obsolete. If, for example, electronic data processing is to be introduced, begin as soon as possible to run down stocks of stationery that will no longer be required.

(*e*) Unless there are good reasons to the contrary, store all stationery centrally, with responsible clerks in charge of keys to cupboards.

(*f*) Issue stationery only against requisitions signed by senior staff.

(*g*) The office supervisor can exercise a simple, but effective, check of stationery wastage by occasionally looking at the waste-paper baskets after the clerks have finished for the day.

2. Buying stationery. The standard methods are:

(*a*) Spot purchase, e.g. from visiting sales representatives. The person placing the order should be a trained buyer, preferably with an Institute of Purchasing and Supply qualification.

(*b*) A system of quotation. This is useful when stationery costs are high.

(*c*) A long-period contract. This is not often used.

(*d*) Tender, i.e. advertising in newspapers and trade journals to invite quotations for a long period supply. This is used mostly by local authorities working to an annual budget.

(*e*) A large volume of modern stationery is used in electronic data processing and not all of it is standard: hence the supplier of the computer will normally provide the specialised stationery.

3. The major buying factors. These are:

(*a*) Buy in sufficient quantities to obtain bulk discount.

(*b*) Consider the cost of storage space. Note the technique, used at ICI, of determining the ideal buying quantity which will equate the administrative buying cost with the storage cost, thus minimising the total acquisition cost of the goods.

(*c*) Obtain from the administrator the pattern of demand from the departments for the various stationery, e.g. the registration department will require large supplies of dividend warrants and tax vouchers at specified times during the year.

(*d*) Price, both current and estimated future price.

(*e*) Quality, relative to purpose. Note the Stock Exchange requirement, *interalia*, that the paper for securities and coupons must be first-class bond or banknote paper containing a water-mark of the printer.

(*f*) Keep within the stationery budget.

4. Stationery storage.

(*a*) Keep the stationery stockroom clean, dry and well-lit.

(*b*) The keys to the stationery stockroom should be held by a responsible clerk in charge.

(c) Orderly arrangement of stationery is essential. Neat stacking on shelves, with clear labelling, and re-ordering time, function of demand pattern and lead time, being shown on coloured cards pinned to the front of the shelves.

5. Issues of stationery.

(a) Devise and rigorously maintain a system of issuing stationery involving minimum delay for those requiring it.

(b) Issue stationery only at specified times and only on presentation of numbered requisitions signed by authorised officials.

(c) Receipt of stationery should be acknowledged in writing by the department requisitioning it.

6. Stationery stock records. In view of the high cost of large stationery stocks it is desirable to record both the amount and the value of stock received and issued, and to integrate stationery costs with the cost accounts.

7. Economies in stationery.

(a) Clerks in charge of stationery must thoroughly understand the types and weights and relative prices of paper, e.g. the distinction between bond and bank.

(b) Do not allow departments to build up their own stocks, thus weakening control at the centre.

(c) Charge each department with stationery issued to it.

(d) If the company is large enough to have its own printing department, devise and print necessary forms.

(e) Convert obsolete stationery into scribbling pads for the use of staff.

(f) If practicable have used stationery re-cycled.

PROGRESS TEST 35

1. It is reported to you that the typing pool always orders two-coloured ribbons. What investigations should you make? **(1)**

2. What are the standard methods of buying stationery? **(2)**

3. What are the possible disadvantages of buying stationery in large quantities in order to enjoy bulk discount? **(3)**

4. What special provisions should be made for departments subject to Stock Exchange regulations? **(3)**

5. Describe an effective method of storing and issuing stationery. **(4, 5)**

6. What steps would you take to encourage the utmost economy of stationery by the staff? **(7)**

CHAPTER XXXVI

Prevention of Fraud

1. Prevention of fraud. This term means:

(*a*) the prevention of theft, i.e. taking property;

(*b*) embezzlement, i.e. unlawful appropriation of cash;

(*c*) forgery, i.e. falsification of documents; and

(*d*) falsification of accounts.

The areas most vulnerable to theft and embezzlement are stores, and cashier's and wages departments. Falsification of documents may occur at any stage of clerical routine, e.g. the forgery of a superior's signature to a cheque, petty cash voucher, stores requisition, or permit to enter a bonded warehouse. The malpractice of teeming and lading is always a possibility when a clerk, or two or more clerks, acting in collusion, divert funds from one account to another in order temporarily to cover embezzled funds. The practice, not necessarily for dishonest purpose, is sometimes called window-dressing.

2. Methods of prevention. Two specific methods of prevention of fraud are:

(*a*) internal check;

(*b*) internal audit.

Neither system, separately, or together is infallible. The following major additional precautions should be taken:

(*c*) Select staff of integrity. The importance of correct recruitment procedure cannot be over-emphasised.

(*d*) Provide good working conditions, realistic promotion prospects and pay good salaries.

(*e*) Be alert to the temptations which young married people, with heavy monthly mortgage payments, face when handling company property and cash.

(*f*) Take note of any gambling going on among the staff.

(*g*) Take out fidelity insurance policies against the risk of fraud, notably that involving large sums of money and that of unauthorised disclosure of the employer's confidential commercial and technical information, e.g. Bentley's code, or a secret chemical formula.

3. Internal check. This involves a logical application of the economic principle of the division of labour, whereby office systems are so arranged, and clerical staff are so allocated to the systems, that they are self-regulating, and there is a continuing automatic check on the work.

There is no standard method of internal check, great variations occurring in practice, although a principle common to all uses is that no one person has responsibility for all aspects of a business transaction, e.g. the purchase of goods on credit and the payment for them involves no fewer than four book-keeping entries, together with many associated entries in the buying department and stores records. The allocation of responsibility for these entries among several clerks will ensure that:

(*a*) The risk of fraud and embezzlement is diminished;

(*b*) the work of one person or section is checked independently by another person or section.

4. The purposes of internal check. These are:

(*a*) to prevent fraud;

(*b*) to detect fraud that has already occurred;

(*c*) to check the efficiency of the office systems, and to recommend, where necessary, any changes in routine deemed desirable, e.g. following recent introduction of new EEC regulations;

(*d*) to fix responsibility for clerical acts, defaults or omissions;

(*e*) to assist in the supervision of staff;

(*f*) partly to anticipate, and thereby to lessen, the work of the internal audit department.

5. Examples of internal check.

(*a*) *Proper division, and clear definition of, tasks and responsibilities.*

(*b*) *Proper design of forms.*

(*i*) A particular set of forms should be numbered consecutively, and the serial numbers should be noted by the clerk in charge of the stationery cupboard.

(*ii*) The printer of the forms should be asked to give a certificate of the exact numbers of the sheets or forms supplied against a given order.

(*iii*) Where statutory books, e.g. register of members, register of charges, minute books, proper books of account, etc., are kept in loose-leaf form, adequate precautions must be taken to prevent fraud, such as the removal of a leaf and the substitution of a false record.

(*iv*) The chairman of a meeting should initial every page of the minutes in addition to dating and signing the minutes themselves.

(*c*) *Safeguarding of assets*, e.g. by separating the cashier from the book-keeper.

(*d*) *Rotating employees from job to job.* If it is known that it is company policy to do this at comparatively short notice, the temptation to steal and repay later, undetected, is thereby reduced. Similarly, once the annual holiday dates have been agreed with the office supervisor, no individual should be permitted, at short notice, to vary the dates without giving a satisfactory reason.

(*e*) *Use of controls*, e.g. control or total accounts are kept in an accounts system involving many ledgers: thus, posting errors are localised to the ledgers in which they occur. Strict control is therefore exercised over many ledger clerks by the supervisor.

A simple, but effective, check of calculations, notably addition and multiplication, is the "casting out of nines" method, illustrated as follows.

An invoice clerk extended 84 articles at £3.14 each as £262.76. If it is required to verify this product in the conventional manner, the checker must repeat the calculation. If his result differs from £262.76, then one of three events has occurred.

(*i*) the invoice clerk is wrong and the checker is right, or
(*ii*) the invoice clerk is right and the checker is wrong, or
(*iii*) they are both wrong.

If the checker, however, applies the "casting out of nines" method, he need not repeat the calculation, for the check, as follows, is independent of the method by which the product was obtained.

(*i*) Cast nines out of 84:

$$8 + 4 = 12$$
$$\text{and } 1 + 2 = 3$$
$$= \text{check figure of the multiplier.}$$

(*ii*) Cast nines out of 3.14:

$$3 + 1 + 4 = 8$$
$$= \text{check figure of the multiplicand.}$$

(*iii*) Multiply together the two derived check figures:

$$3 \times 8 = 24$$
$$\text{and } 2 + 4 = 6$$
$$= \text{check figure of the product.}$$

(*iv*) If the alleged product is correct, its check figure must also be 6.

(*v*) But:

$$2 + 6 + 2 + 7 + 6 = 23$$
$$\text{and } 2 + 3 = 5$$

Note that in deriving the check figures, the figure 9, or any combination of figures totalling 9, may be omitted, thus shortening the operation, e.g. in the above addition, $2 + 7$ may be omitted, and the check figure will still be 5.

(*vi*) The invoice clerk's extension is, therefore, incorrect.

It is to be noted, however, that agreement of check figures does not necessarily prove a calculation correct, since the "nines" check is insensitive to errors attributable to compensating errors or transposition of figures, although these types of error are infrequent. If greater assurance is required, higher check figures such as 11, 13, 17 or 19 should be applied. The decimalisation of English currency greatly simplified the application of these higher check numbers.

(*f*) *Adequate safeguards for the keeping and issuing of the business assets.*

(*i*) Regular use of the night-safe at the company's bank.

(*ii*) The employment of security services for the transit of cash and other valuables.

(*iii*) Important documents such as title-deeds, insurance policies, confidential technical formulae, etc., must be kept in a safe deposit with the company's banker.

(*iv*) Appropriate insurance policies covering risks to business assets and risk of loss of profit following a fire must be maintained and checked regularly to verify that the premiums are sufficient to produce necessary funds to replace an asset affected by inflation.

(*g*) *Keeping petty cash and postal accounts on the imprest system.* The clerk in charge is handed cash, on the first day of every month, equivalent to the amount which he disbursed in the preceding month.

(*h*) *Cancellation of used documents*, especially purchase invoices and petty cash vouchers.

(*i*) *Insist that every piece of paper entering, or leaving, the office be properly dated.*

(j) Second signature on cheques. Cheques must be supported by properly authenticated vouchers.

(k) *Keys to safes, loose-leaf statutory books and to the company's seal must be in duplicate form,* held by senior members of staff. Duplicate keys must be held by the company's banker or solicitor.

(l) Where EDP is in operation, the programme will include a rigorous check on its own output. Note however, the risk of a costly error, fraudulent or negligent, by the systems analyst or by the computer programmer. A special type of insurance policy is available to cover this risk.

6. Internal audit. This is a special branch of a business, (normally the responsibility of the chief accountant), which carries out a continuous audit on the organisation's own staff.

(a) This audit consists of a systematic examination of all books of account and records, notably those of the buying department, cost and wages departments, and the stores.

(b) The audit will exercise a rigorous check on the spending of departmental budgets.

(c) Internal check is devised to operate as a self-regulating means of control, whereas internal audit is performed by special staff, who are often professionally qualified, and it is a continuous process.

(d) Internal audit covers the same ground as the external audit required by statute for companies, although internal auditors are responsible through the chief accountant to the board of directors, whereas external auditors have a statutory duty to report to the shareholders.

(e) The internal auditors can assist, and save the time of, the external auditors, and therefore part of the fees payable for the external statutory audit.

7. Receipt of cash. Steps to prevent fraud include the following.

(a) Use cash registers wherever possible, although it is still necessary to trust assistants.

(b) Separate the receipt of cash from selling activities: goods must not be released from store until evidence of payment is produced, e.g. a sales note stamped "paid" by the cashier.

(c) Bank cash as often as possible and late in the day.

(d) Give prominent notice to customers that official receipts must be requested when they pay.

(e) Do not let the cashier keep the sales or purchase ledgers.

8. Payment of cash.

(*a*) All debts over £1 to be paid by cheque.

(*b*) All cash payments must be evidenced by signed petty cash vouchers, with invoices or statements attached.

(*c*) Never cash employees' cheques or advance money to them.

9. Receipt of cheques.

(*a*) Immediately on receipt, rubber stamp cheques with a crossing stamp bearing the name of the company's bank.

(*b*) List all cheques when received: total the list and compare it with the bank paying-in book.

(*c*) Do not delay to pay cheques into the bank, to avoid any R/D (refer to drawer) cheques. This is especially relevant when a public issue of a company's shares is over-subscribed.

(*d*) A clerk other than the one keeping the cash book should compile the bank reconciliation statement.

10. Payment by cheque.

(*a*) Use a cheque-writing machine.

(*b*) Write cheques correctly—date, words tallying with figures, giving no possibility of fraudulent insertion of additional figures, and always use cheques with printed crossings.

(*c*) Cheques to be signed only against accompanying certified invoice or authorised voucher.

(*d*) Two signatures to all cheques, in practice, those of a director and the secretary.

(*e*) Cancel the supporting documents and mark on each the number of the cheque.

11. Wage systems.

(*a*) Divide the duties of calculating wages from those of drawing money from the bank and paying it out.

(*b*) The internal auditor should sometimes, at very short notice, replace the person who normally pays out the wages.

(*c*) Use pay numbers and enter names and numbers of new employees on the payroll only by order of the personnel department.

(*d*) Similarly, alter wage-rates, bonus payments, etc., only on express instructions of the personnel department or other authority, e.g. the cost office.

(*e*) Regularly check the pay-roll against:

    (*i*) time cards;

(*ii*) time sheets;

(*iii*) P11 deduction cards.

(*f*) Where the employees have agreed in writing to waive their legal right to be paid in legal tender, pay wages by cheque.

12. Stock.

(*a*) All goods sold on credit should be released from store only against an official order from the customer.

(*b*) All credit deliveries must be approved by the credit control department for all items exceeding, say, £5.

(*c*) Take stock regularly; use random sampling methods to take spot checks.

(*d*) Use a perpetual inventory system, entering bin-cards as a check on stock records (*see* Fig. 7).

(*e*) Inventory records are among the most useful and widely applied uses of electronic data processing.

Part No.	·SCM/1175		*Maximum:	40 gross
Description	Sparking plug		*Minimum:	15 gross
Date	Reference	No. received. gr.	No. issued gr.	Balance gr.
1978				
Jan. 1	B/f			23.5
16	Order 3497	15		38.5
20	Requis. 476		6	32.5
23	" 517		5	27.5
27	" 749		8.5	19
Feb 7	Order 5113	20		39

FIG. 7   *A specimen bin card.*

*Maximum and minimum stock levels are derived from experience of the pattern of demand for the stock and from the lead time, i.e. the period between placing an order for the stock and the date of receipt of the goods.

13. Sales invoicing.

(*a*) Use pre-numbered invoices and check their serial numbers when posting to the sales ledger.

(*b*) Prepare sales invoice, advice note, transport advice, export documents, etc., all simultaneously by using continuous stationery and an accounting machine.

(*c*) Do not dispatch goods without the relevant documents. Correct dating of documents is vital in this context.

14. New techniques.

Word-processing and microcomputers greatly strengthen the ability of an office administrator to prevent and to detect fraud, especially in relation to the payroll and to stock records. As described in XXVI, the instant retrieval of, e.g. the stock position of a particular item, and the display of the figures on the VDU facilitates the "spot check" at random.

PROGRESS TEST 36

1. What aspects of business should be considered in connection with the prevention of fraud?   (**1**)

2. What are the limits of internal audit and internal check, and what more can be done to prevent fraud?   (**2**)

3. What are the major purposes of internal check?   (**4**)

4. What purpose is served by rotating employees from job to job and by insistence upon keeping the agreed holiday dates?   (**5**)

5. Compare and contrast internal check and internal audit. (**6**)

6. Receipt and payment of cash are a vulnerable source of fraud. Describe the basic methods of prevention.   (**7, 8**)

7. What procedures would you recommend to minimise fraud in the drawing of cheques?   (**10**)

8. What steps ought to be taken to minimise fraud in a wages department?   (**11**)

9. In what way does a bin-card serve to prevent fraud in the stores?   (**12**)

CHAPTER XXXVII

Reports and Minutes

1. Definitions. Confusion between the meanings of reports and minutes is considerable in practice.

(*a*) The word report derives from the Latin *reportare*, to bring back, i.e. a report is written by a person who has investigated facts or circumstances and "brings back" the results of his investigation. For example a specialist in, say, taxation, is co-opted to a committee and instructed to investigate and report on a taxation problem affecting the company.

(*b*) The word minutes means a short, concise record of what was *done*, not what was *said*, at a meeting. The keeping of minutes of:

(*i*) company meetings;
(*ii*) board meetings;
(*iii*) meetings of managers

is a statutory obligation (s. 145 (1) Companies Act 1948).

2. The major kinds of report.

(*a*) Informal reports written by individuals inside a business on special, i.e. ad hoc, occasions.

(*b*) Formal reports made by committees to their parent bodies.

(*c*) Statutory reports required by law.

(*d*) Routine reports, perhaps with printed headings, which relate to a set of data at regular intervals.

3. The two kinds of minute.

(*a*) Minutes of resolution, e.g. "It was resolved *that* the registered office of the company be situate at 15, High Street, Eastingtown".

(*b*) Minutes of narration, e.g. "The secretary was authorised to purchase books and stationery necessary for the company's business".

4. Importance of reports. Reports are a means of upward communication in business, so that feedback is provided for management which enables it to test or modify company policies. A

200 THREE: RECORDS AND GENERAL SERVICES

well-drafted report is a stimulus to action: a badly-drafted one often "darkens counsel by words without knowledge".

5. Qualities of writer of reports.

(*a*) Knowledge of the subject.

(*b*) Powers of observation and analytical ability—to apply "Occam's razor" ruthlessly, that is, to reject all unnecessary detail, and, in particular, loose and ambiguous verbiage. e.g. "action is needed" is better than "something ought to be done about it"; "I will verify it" is better than "I will check up on it".

(*c*) Sound, unbiased judgment.

(*d*) Accuracy in expression—the test of communication is understanding.

(*e*) Knowledge of report-writing technique.

6. Form of a report.

(*a*) Address the report to a definite reader or body of readers.

(*b*) Except when the report is informal, address the reader(s) as "Sir" or "Gentlemen".

(*c*) Give the report a short, clear title.

(*d*) Always state the terms of reference, that is, the scope of the enquiry and by whom it was commissioned.

(*e*) Arrange the body of the report in logical sequence, with headed paragraphs.

(*f*) Any recommendations should be marked as such and included either at the end of relevant parts of the report, or all together in an appendix.

(*g*) Always date and sign a report.

7. Technique of report writing.

(*a*) The report must be objective, that is, factual, and the outcome of observation, experiment, inspection and research.

(*b*) It must not be subjective, expressing ideas and opinions. The reader should form his opinions from the facts adduced.

(*c*) The style must be suited to the reader. Therefore technical and legal expressions should be explained if the report is addressed to laymen.

(*d*) Tables, charts and graphs accompanying the report must always be titled and explained.

(*e*) It is particularly important to state the source of any statistics quoted, and to ensure that graphs do not mislead the readers.

PROGRESS TEST 37

1. State the difference between a report and minutes. (**1**)

2. What are: (*a*) the major kinds of report? (*b*) the two kinds of minute? (**1**)

3. What are the basic parts of a report? (**4**)

4. What, in your opinion, is the basic requirement of report writers? (**5**)

APPENDIX I

Bibliography

Neuner, J. J. W., *Administrative Office Management*, 6th edition, South Western Publishing Co., 1972.

Chappel, R. T. and Read, W. L., *Business Communications*, 4th edition, Macdonald & Evans, 1979.

Dale, J. R., *The Clerk in Industry*, Liverpool University Press, 1962.

The Design of Forms in Government Departments, 3rd edition, HMSO, 1972.

Department of Health and Social Security, *Employers' Guide to National Insurance Contributions*, HMSO, 1977.

Board of Inland Revenue, Employers' Guide to PAYE, HMSO, 1980.

Munro Fraser, J., *Employment Interviewing*, 5th edition, Macdonald & Evans, 1978.

How to Design a Procedure, 2nd edition, IAM, 1974.

Ashton, F., *Mechanised Accounting*, Macdonald & Evans, 1973.

Gartside, L., *Modern Business Correspondence*, 3rd edition, Macdonald & Evans, 1976.

Denyer, J. C., revised Shaw, J., *Office Management*, 5th edition, Macdonald & Evans, 1980.

Milward, G. E. (ed.), *Organization and Methods*, 2nd edition, Macmillan, 1967.

Northcott, C., *Personnel Management*, Pitman.

Personnel Management—a Bibliography, Parts 1, 2 and 3, IPM, 1973–75.

Personnel Selection Testing, BIM, 1972.

Post Office, *Post Office Guide*, HMSO, 1980.

Brech, E. F. L., *Principles and Practice of Management*, 3rd edition, Longman, 1975.

Procedure Charts for Administrative Work, 2nd edition, IAM, 1972.

McCabe, Helen M. and Popham, Estelle L., *Word-processing*, Harcourt Brace, Jovanovich Inc., New York.

H. M. Customs and Excise, *Value Added Tax*, HMSO, 1980.

Cemach, H. P., *Work Study in the Office*, 4th edition, Applied Science Publishers, 1969.

NOTE: The bulk of the material involved in the updating of this book was drawn from various professional journals and from national newspapers. In every case I have paraphrased the originals.

Examination Technique

Office administration is a wide subject and the questions set on it are of many types, since its subject-matter ranges from organisation and personnel to electronic computers and filing systems, the purchase of stationery and the prevention of fraud.

Four types of question. Questions on office machines are basically of four types:

(*a*) Describe the operation or principles of operation (not mechanical operation).

(*b*) Discuss the advantages of a particular machine.

(*c*) List the different uses of a particular machine; and

(*d*) Discuss the factors to consider when purchasing and installing such a machine.

Regarding personnel, as well as the basic theory of interviewing, promotion, etc., students should be prepared to be able to reproduce application forms, personnel records, staff reports, etc., which are featured in the main textbook *Office Management* (Macdonald & Evans).

Examination hints

1. First read the question two or three times to make sure you understand precisely what is required.

2. Where a question has auxiliary questions, mark on the examination paper the number of points to be covered.

EXAMPLE: "Describe what is meant by a central dictating system. ① What are its advantages, ② and in what circumstances would you recommend the installation of such a system?" ③

3. If a question appears to have two interpretations, include answers to both in your answer, so that you are sure of getting half right.

4. Before actually writing your examination answer, jot down on a piece of scrap paper the main points you intend including in your answer. *Do your thinking first.*

5. Write your answer in short sentences, in simple English; and keep the length of paragraphs short.

6. While the statement of principles, factors, etc., is important, quote examples to emphasise the points you wish to make.

7. *If the question is suitable*, e.g. if it requests you to "state the advantages of" or "enumerate the factors in", then it is advisable to tabulate your answer.

8. But if a question asks you to "Discuss the centralisation of office services," it is imperative that a discussion kind of essay be written, i.e. put points for and against in each paragraph, and *not* a listing of the advantages and disadvantages of centralisation.

9. Answer the question, the whole question, and nothing but the question. Remember the more you write, the greater the chance of contradicting yourself.

EXAMPLE: If asked "How would you redesign the lay-out of an office?" this requires an outline of the practical steps to be taken with new lay-out. Factors of lay-out should be mentioned only as the deciding factors in the arrangement. It would not be necessary to list the factors.

10. Prepare for questions involving matters of law, such as the Offices, Shops and Railway Premises Act 1963, or the Employment Protection Act 1975, by a careful study of their major provisions and their implications for office administration.

11. Remember that, in the context of office machinery and equipment, the best textbook is the current issue of the professional journals. Read the articles and the advertisements about new ideas, miss no opportunity to study the equipment in your own office and make sure you attend all available exhibitions of office machinery.

Q. *In designing a payroll system, what measures would you make to prevent fraud?*

A. The preparation of a payroll and the payment of wages are vulnerable to many types of fraud, some of them highly ingenious. Collusion among wage-office clerks and between office and factory: the creation of "dummy" employees and falsification or records are common in practice. The need for rigorous internal audit following the adoption of the payroll system is, therefore, essential.

Preparation of the payroll.

1. Divide the duties among different members of staff (or among different departments in a large business; e.g. the wages department

itself calculates the basic wage from the time-cards or similar records of hours worked, while the cost office calculates productivity bonus payments).

2. Compare time-sheets and time-cards with Deductions Working Sheets (P11 New), issued by the Inland Revenue.

3. Use one of the many "softwares" with Database available for electronic data processing of the payroll. Retrieval of data from store and its display on the VDU greatly aids the detection of fraud and error.

4. Insist that pay-clerks take their holidays on the agreed dates and do not change at short-notice without giving a satisfactory reason to the supervisor.

5. Frequent "spot-checks" should be carried out.

Payment of wages

1. Encourage employees to authorise (in writing) the payment of wages by cheque, traders' credit or by mandate to credit accounts at the branch of a bank named by an individual employee.

2. If cash has to be drawn from the bank, employ the services of Securicor, or other cash-carrying agency (if the amount of cash involved is large enough to justify payment for the service).

3. Clerks other than those preparing the payroll should hand the wage packets to the employees. Without notice, the supervisor should occasionally replace the regular clerks himself.

4. On no account should an employee be allowed to draw wages for a colleague: foremen are sometimes allowed to draw wages for absent employees of their section.

5. Some companies require employees to sign for their wages. This is facilitated by handing the following to each person a few hours before payment:

(*a*) the clock card showing the calculation of the wage on the back.

(*b*) two copies (using carbon) showing date, name, clock number, total wage, deductions and net wage.

Any queries can be settled before the actual payment and adjustments noted for the following pay-roll. The employee signs one copy of (*b*) and hands it to the pay-clerk in exchange for the wage packet. He retains the other copy. There are many variations of the system in practice.

6. Any wage-packets not claimed must be rigorously accounted

for. In practice, many of these packets contain tax refunds for absent employees. Persons claiming these after the payout are required to submit authorisation from the employee.

7. Verify that adequate insurance has been taken out, and is being maintained, against loss caused by fraud.

Test Papers

Do not attempt these papers until you have thoroughly mastered the course and are able to answer all the Progress Tests satisfactorily. Do each paper under strict examination conditions, bearing in mind the hints on examination technique in Appendix II (the papers are adapted from actual ones set by the Institute of Administrative Management (1) and the Institute of Chartered Secretaries and Administrators (2)).

Paper 1

Time allowed: 3 hours
Answer any FIVE questions
All questions carry equal marks

1. Describe briefly *four* of the following and give an example of the use of each:

Typewriter with variable type   Continuous stationery
Micro-film   Addressing machine
Manifold posting board   Visible card index

2. What method of duplicating would you recommend for each of the following jobs? Give your reasons.

(*a*) six copies of a multi-coloured sales chart;

(*b*) 2000 copies of a form in triplicate to be filled in by sales representatives;

(*c*) 1000 copies of a price list; and

(*d*) 20 copies of an agenda paper for a works committee meeting.

3. Name and describe the functions of the five basic components of an electronic computer.

4. What are the advantages and disadvantages of audio-typing pools?

5. What steps would you take to ensure good working conditions in an office?

6. In designing a payroll system, what provisions would you make to prevent fraud?

7. Name and describe briefly six machines or devices which can be used to speed the handling of incoming and/or outgoing mail in a postal section.

8. Describe a sales invoicing system from the receipt of a customer's order to the posting of the sales ledger account.

Paper 2

Time allowed: 3 hours
Answer any SIX questions
All questions carry equal marks

1. The purpose of the office has been defined as the providing of a service of communication and record. Amplify and comment on this definition.

2. (*a*) List the salient features of each of the following methods of duplicating:

(*i*) Stencil
(*ii*) Spirit hectograph
(*iii*) Offset litho

and

(*b*) State which of these methods you would recommend to reproduce the following:

(*i*) Six copies of a multi-coloured chart.
(*ii*) 100 copies of the agenda of a meeting.
(*iii*) 2000 forms which will later be filled in by pen and ink.

3. Name four methods of classifying filing and give an example of the circumstances in which each method might best be adopted.

4. Describe briefly the functions of *four* of the following machines used in connection with punched cards:

| Tabulator | Punch | Summary punch |
| Collator | Interpreter | Reproducer |

5. Describe briefly a system of job grading and state the benefits to be gained from its use from the point of view of: (*a*) management, and (*b*) staff.

6. What are the advantages and disadvantages of typing pools?

7. What are the principal causes of errors in clerical work and how would you try to *prevent* them?

8. List and describe briefly the steps you would take in planning an office organisation.

9. Describe briefly *four* of the following, giving examples of their uses:

Manifold posting-board   Suspension filing
Adding/listing machine   Wheel index
Heat transfer copying   Addressing plate

Index